MOONCHILDREN

MOONCHILDREN

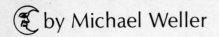 by Michael Weller

A DELTA BOOK

A DELTA BOOK
Published by
Dell Publishing Co., Inc.
750 Third Avenue
New York, New York 10017

Originally published in Great Britain under the title CANCER by
Faber & Faber Limited.

Published by arrangement with Delacorte Press
New York, New York
Printed in the United States of America
First Delta printing—April 1972

introduction

MOONCHILDREN are a troop of college kids who live together in one of those lyrically sloppy rooming-house rooms that buzz with the myth of total freedom. "God is Cool," says a sign on the ancient refrigerator, empty milk bottles line every horizontal surface, the stash of pot lies peacefully beneath a seedy sprig of flowers, the cat occupies a fourth dimension of independence inside her box. It is five or six years ago, commencement is coming, the Beatles are blooming, peace marches are deploying, Kathy and Bob are still making it but Kathy is eying Dick, who is (maybe) making it with a prof's wife, and Ruth's long dark hair swings with sadness for all of this. And then there are Mike and Cootie, really smart guys who have developed a positively Wittgensteinian genius to turn any situation into a put-on—to the tenth factor and beyond. And Norman is so busy studying that literally every item in the above is lost upon him—he is so straight he can't even be put on.

It sounds insane to say that this household is somehow like Shaw's Heartbreak House, like Chekhov's country houses filled with half-cocooned butterflies. But Michael Weller's play is so sensitive, so intelligent, so alert to the puppies beneath the skin of these nonstop but transfixed young people that the comparison forces itself. Along with David Rabe he is part of a new generation of American playwrights who work from an absolute psychic authenticity, who have perfect pitch for the microtones of these strange young nervous systems who are going to inherit the anguished earth.

Moonchildren is a young man's play, and yet almost every time one sniffs a gaucherie coming up, it pivots and shifts and snaps into a brilliancy. This quality is very much involved with the idea and action of the put-on, an evasive concept that Weller uses with devastating insight to capture the moral dilemma of his generation. These kids know that meaningful life has been kidnaped, and its abducted energy has left them in a kind of cosmic terror that they stave off with a complex ritual of wiseguy voodoo that Weller uses in many different ways, working delicately through scenes of mad comedy toward his climax of desolation. This is an extraordinarily subtle play, registering the true temperature of "issues"—the war, the generation gap— at their spiritual center.

JACK KROLL

MOONCHILDREN received its first American production at ARENA STAGE, Washington, D.C., November 1971, prior to the Broadway opening in February 1972.

ARENA STAGE
Thomas C. Fichandler, *Executive Director*
Zelda Fichandler, *Producing Director*

MOONCHILDREN
by MICHAEL WELLER

Produced by ZELDA FICHANDLER
Directed by ALAN SCHNEIDER
Setting by WILLIAM RITMAN
Costumes by MARJORIE SLAIMAN
Lighting by VANCE SORRELLS
Production Manager: HUGH LESTER
Technical Director: HENRY R. GORFEIN

By arrangement with Martin Rosen, Nepenthe Productions, Ltd., and The Royal Court Theater

the cast
(IN ORDER OF SPEAKING)

THE STUDENTS

Mike—KEVIN CONWAY
Ruth—MAUREEN ANDERMAN
Cootie (Mel)—EDWARD HERRMANN
Norman—CHRISTOPHER GUEST
Dick—STEPHEN COLLINS
Kathy—JILL EIKENBERRY
Bob Rettie (Job)—JAMES WOODS
Shelly—CARA DUFF-MAC CORMICK

THE OTHERS

Ralph—DONEGAN SMITH
Mr. Willis—ROBERT PROSKY
Lucky—RONALD MC LARTY
Bream—HOWARD WITT
Effing—TED HANNAN
Uncle Murry—RUSSELL CARR
Milkman—MARK ROBINSON

synopsis of scenes

ACT ONE

Scene 1. An evening in early fall
Scene 2. A few weeks later. Morning.
Scene 3. That afternoon.
Scene 4. A November evening.

ACT TWO

Scene 5. Morning, just before Christmas vacation.
Scene 6. Late spring, before graduation.
Scene 7. The following afternoon.

*The place is a student apartment in an American
university town.*
The time is around 1965–66

ACT ONE

ACT ONE

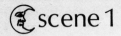scene 1

[*The stage is dark. You can't see anything.*]

MIKE
I heard something. She definitely made a noise.

RUTH
Shut up.

MIKE
I'm telling you, I know the noise they make. That was
it.

RUTH
For chrissakes, be quiet. You keep talking and she'll
know we're here.

COOTIE
I was just thinking. I read somewhere about how they
can see in the dark.

RUTH

I never read that.

COOTIE

No shit, I read they got these hundreds of thousands of millions of tiny, submicroscopic, photosensitive cells in each eyeball, so when it gets dark they can just turn on these cells and see like it was daytime.

MIKE

He's right, Ruth. Hey, Cootie, you're right. I remember reading that in a back issue of the *Vertebrate Review*.

COOTIE

That's it, that's the one. Special eyeball issue.

MIKE

Yeah, yeah. July.

RUTH

You guys must be pretty stupid if you believe that. What do you think they have whiskers for? The whole point of whiskers in the first place is so you can get around in the dark. That's why they stick out so far, so you don't bump into things. Chairs and refrigerators and that.

MIKE

Hey, shhhhh. I think she's starting.

RUTH

Well, you're the one that got me going about whiskers in the first place, so don't tell me shhhhh.

MIKE

OK, OK, I'm sorry, OK?

RUTH

So shut up if she's starting.

COOTIE

[*Pause*] How many kittens can they have at any one session?

MIKE

There's a recorded case of thirty-eight.

RUTH

Shhhh, for chrissakes.

COOTIE

What I want to know is how are we gonna see her when she starts giving birth?

RUTH

Jesus, how stupid can you get? We'll turn on the light.

5

COOTIE

Yeah, but the whole thing is how do we know when to turn on the light? Like, what if we're too early?

MIKE

Or too late?

COOTIE

Yeah, what if we're too late?

MIKE

Or right in the middle . . .

COOTIE

Holy shit, yeah, what if we flip on the old lights when she's halfway through a severe uterine contraction? She'll go apeshit and clamp up and kill the kitten. And if the kitty gets really lucky and wiggles free it'll grow up into a pretty fucked-up animal.

MIKE

We're sowing the seeds of a neurotic adult cathood . . .

COOTIE

. . . doo-wah, doo-wah . . .

RUTH

Hey, shut up, you guys, willya? Willya shut up?

COOTIE

We're just pointing out that's a shitty way to start life.

RUTH

I know the noise, all right?

MIKE

I think there's probably a more scientific way to watch a cat give birth.

RUTH

Everybody shut the fuck up.

[*A long pause.*]

NORMAN

How much longer are you guys gonna have the lights out?

COOTIE

Jesus Christ, Norman, why do you have to go creeping up like that? We forgot you were even in here.

NORMAN

I'm not creeping up. I'm just sitting here. Maybe you didn't notice when you came in, but I was reading this book. I mean, I thought you were only gonna have the lights out for maybe a few minutes or something, but you've already been in here for about an hour and . . .

and I really can't read very well with the lights off. I
mean . . . you know . . .

COOTIE
Norman, you can't rush a cat when it's giving birth.
You try to rush a cat in those circumstances and you
come smack up against nature.

MIKE
Norman . . .

NORMAN
What?

MIKE
Don't fight nature, Norman.

NORMAN
I'm not. I'm just trying to read this book.

COOTIE
[*Pause*] Is it a good book?

RUTH
For chrissakes, what's the matter with everyone?

NORMAN
I don't know. It's a pretty good book. I don't follow all

of it. It's written in a funny kind of way so you forget a
lot of it right after you've read it. A lot of guys in the
mathematics department say it's pretty good. I don't
know though.

RUTH

Hey Norman, can't you go to your room if you want to
read?

NORMAN

I don't want to.

COOTIE

Why not, Norman?

MIKE

Yeah, why do you want to creep around in here being
all spooky and everything when you could just go to
your room and read, huh?

NORMAN

I don't know.

COOTIE

We may be in here for hours and hours, Norman.
Maybe even all night. The whole operation from initial

labor to the biting off of the umbilical cord could very easily take an entire night. [*Pause*] Norman?

NORMAN
All night, huh?

COOTIE
You never know.

RUTH
Brother, you try to get a few guys to shut up for a little while . . .

MIKE
[*Loud*] C'mon, c'mon, hey everybody, let's have a little quiet around here. I don't want to see anyone panic and lose their heads and start running in all different directions knocking down passersby and trampling on innocent women and children.

RUTH
I swear to Christ, Mike, if you don't shut up I'll kill you.

MIKE
OK.

[*At this point, the hall door opens and the kitchen is lit up a little.* DICK *is standing in the doorway trying to see into the dark, where* NORMAN *is sitting at a round kitchen table with a book by him and* RUTH, MIKE, *and* COOTIE *are crouched around a cardboard carton with a hole in it.* NORMAN *grabs up his book to take advantage of the crack of light.* DICK *just stands there.* RUTH *and* COOTIE *speak on top of each other.*]

RUTH

Hey, c'mon, shut the door, Dick.

COOTIE

Shut the fucking door.

MIKE

[*After a pause*] We'd really like you to shut the door, Richard.

[DICK *shuts the door and everything goes black again. A moment later it all lights up again because* DICK *has just opened the icebox and it's the kind that has an automatic light inside. So now we see* DICK *squatting in front of the icebox while the others watch him, except for* NORMAN *who's really trying like mad to read. You can see the kitchen pretty clearly now. The icebox is very old, dating from the time when electricity was replacing the iceman. It's just a box on legs with one of those barrel-shaped coolers with vents on top. You maybe can't see it yet, but on the door of the icebox there's a large inscription that reads "GOD IS*

*COOL." Stacked neatly against one wall are eight
hundred sixteen empty two-quart milk bottles, layer
upon layer with planks between each level. It's a
deliberate construction. There's a huge copper stack
heater in one corner by the sink, and it has a safety
valve at the top with a copper tube coming out of it
and snaking into the sink. The floor is vinyl, in
imitation cork, alternating light and dark, but the
conspicuous thing about this floor is that it's only
half-finished. Where the cork tiles end there is a border
of black tar, by now hard, and then wooden floor in
broad plank. Around the kitchen table are six chairs,
all from different sets. Various posters on the wall, but
none as conspicuous as a map of Europe on the wall
where the telephone hangs. The sink is full of dirty
dishes. There is a pad hanging by the icebox, and a
pencil. Everyone uses the kitchen in a special way. So*
DICK *is squatting in front of the open icebox.*]

RUTH

That's very cute, Richard.

MIKE

C'mon, shut the fucking icebox. We were in here first.

NORMAN

I was reading when you guys came in.

[DICK *turns to them, looks, then turns back to the
icebox.*]

COOTIE

Dick, in my humble opinion you're a miserable cunt and a party pooper.

DICK

[*Standing*] All right, now listen. This afternoon I went down to the Star Supermarket and got myself four dozen frozen hamburgers. Now that's forty-eight hamburgers, and I only had two of them for dinner tonight.

RUTH

And you never washed up.

MIKE

Hey, Dick, are those Star hamburgers any good?

DICK

Listen, I should have forty-six hamburgers, and when I counted just now there was only forty-three. Three hamburgers in one night. And for your information I've been keeping track of my hamburgers since the beginning of the semester. There's almost fifty hamburgers I can't account for.

COOTIE

Jesus, Dick, you should have said something before this.

MIKE

Yeah, Dick, you had all them hamburger thefts on your mind, you should have let it out. It's no good keeping quiet about something like that.

DICK

Look, I'm not about to make a stink about a couple of hamburgers here and there, but Jesus Christ, almost sixty of them. I'm putting it down on common stock and we're gonna all pay for it.

[DICK *turns on the light.*]

RUTH

Dick, willya turn out the light, please.

DICK

I'm sorry, but I've lost too many hamburgers. I'm putting down for four dozen.

[DICK *goes to the pad on the wall and makes an entry.*]

RUTH

Now willya turn the light out?

DICK

[*Examining list*] Shit, who put peanut butter down on common stock?

MIKE

I did. I got a jar of chunky last Thursday and when I opened it on Saturday somebody'd already been in there. I didn't eat all that chunky myself.

DICK

Well I never had your peanut butter. I'm not paying for it.

MIKE

Well I never had any of your goddamn sixty hamburgers either.

COOTIE

I think I may have had some of that chunky peanut butter. Could you describe your jar of chunky in detail?

MIKE

Elegant little glass jar, beige interior . . ..

[KATHY *enters through the front door, as opposed to the hall door. The hall door leads to everyone's rooms.*]

KATHY

Oh boy, look out for Bob.

[KATHY *starts across the kitchen to the hall door. She carries lots of books in a green canvas waterproof book bag slung over her shoulder.*]

15

RUTH

What's wrong with Bob?

KATHY

He's in a really shitty mood. I've seen the guy act weird before. This is, I don't know, pretty bad, I guess.

MIKE

Where is he?

COOTIE

Yeah, where's Bob?

MIKE

Good old Bob.

COOTIE

Where's good old Bob?

KATHY

And fuck you too. I'm serious.

NORMAN

[*Looking up from his book*] Boy, I really can't absorb very much with everyone talking.

KATHY

We were just sitting there, you know, in Hum 105,

16

and that prick Johnson started in about the old cosmic
equation again.

NORMAN
What's the cosmic equation?

RUTH
So why'd that upset Bob?

KATHY
I don't know. That's the thing . . .

DICK
I bet Bob's responsible for some of my hamburgers. I
notice you and him never go shopping for dinner.

KATHY
It's really weird the way he sort of . . . well, like today,
you know . . . well, I mean, haven't you noticed it?

MIKE
Look, Kathy, you're never gonna find out what's
troubling Bob unless you can get him to admit whether
or not . . . [*Thinking*] . . . well . . .

KATHY
What?

MIKE
Well, if he's been hanging around Lake Kariba.

KATHY
What?

COOTIE
Yeah, that's right, there's an epidemic of schistosomiasis up round Lake Kariba country . . .

KATHY
Oh, you fucking guys . . .

MIKE
Kathy, you don't wanna go ignoring a possibility like that. It can be pretty serious if it isn't treated immediately.

COOTIE
Yeah, there's these giant snails round the marshes that lie in ambush and jump onto passersby.

MIKE
They don't jump.

COOTIE
They do.

MIKE
Catapult.

COOTIE
Oh, yeah.

MIKE
See, they work in teams of two. One of them holds back the blade of grass between his teeth while the other one crawls up onto the end, and on a given signal the holder opens his mouth and . . . thwock . . . right onto you, and you get these microscopic parasites in your bloodstream . . .

COOTIE
And your liver shrivels up . . . you turn yellow . . .

MIKE
You start mixing tenses . . .

COOTIE
Dropping split infinitives and dangling metaphors left, right, and center and . . . and . . .

RUTH
You finished?

COOTIE
You?

MIKE
Yeah, you?

COOTIE
Yeah.

MIKE
We're finished.

KATHY
[*Ignores them*] I know the guy. He's never like this.
He's just . . . Christ, I'm not kidding, he might be
cracking up or something.

[BOB *enters through the front door, carrying his books.*
He looks all right. Everyone stares at him.]

RUTH
Hi, Bob.

MIKE
Hi, Bob.

COOTIE
Hi, Bob.

NORMAN
Hello, Bob.

BOB

[*Pause*] Hi, Mike, Hi, Ruth, Hi, Cootie, hello, Norman.
[*Pause*] Hi, Dick.

DICK

Listen, do you know anything about . . .

BOB

No, I haven't touched your fucking hamburgers.

DICK

Well someone has.

MIKE

How you been, good old Bob?

COOTIE

How's the old liver and the old pancreas and the old
pituitary and the . . .

BOB

Is there any mail?

COOTIE

There's this really big package from Beirut. It took four
guys to get it up the stairs.

MIKE

We think it's a harp.

RUTH

There's a letter in your room.

[BOB *looks at them quizzically, then goes down the hall.* KATHY *follows him.*]

NORMAN

He sure gets a lot of letters. I wonder if he writes a lot?

COOTIE

The thing to do if you want to get a lot of mail is start a chain letter.

NORMAN

How do you do that?

MIKE

You never heard of chain letters?

NORMAN

No.

MIKE

You should've heard of them. They're a great way to

22

get letters. 1 started one once and I think I got about four hundred and eight letters in two months.

COOTIE

If you do it right you're supposed to get a thousand.

MIKE

I would've got a thousand but I moved. The guy that stayed in the apartment got five hundred and ninety-two letters.

COOTIE

You should've left a forwarding address.

MIKE

Shit, I never thought of that.

RUTH

I think Kathy's right. There's definitely something wrong with Bob.

DICK

Yeah, he's out of his fucking mind, that's what's wrong with him.

RUTH

You can talk.

NORMAN

Is that where you write to, say 'n' people and tell them all to write to 'n' people until it . . .

MIKE

Yeah, and you can put something in the letters, like a dollar or two dollars or Band-Aids or a picture of Liberace . . .

RUTH

Jesus Christ, what the hell's wrong with everyone around here?

MIKE

Hey, c'mon, c'mon, let's have a little order around here . . .

RUTH

Stop fucking around. You heard what Kathy said. Something's troubling Bob.

MIKE

So what?

COOTIE

Yeah, fuck Bob.

MIKE

Fuck good old Bob.

NORMAN

Maybe he's worried about the future. [*All look at him*] I mean, you know, maybe he's worried about it. I mean, I don't know him all that well. Just, you know, maybe he's worried about what he's gonna do when, you know, after he graduates and everything.

DICK

He ought to be worried.

MIKE

You bet your ass he oughta be. Same goes for all of you guys. You oughta be worried, Dick. Cootie, you oughta be worried. I oughta be worried. I am. I'm fucking petrified. You watch what happens at the graduation ceremony. There's gonna be this line of green military buses two miles long parked on the road outside and they're gonna pick us up and take us to Vietnam and we'll be walking around one day in the depths of the rain forest looking out for wily enemy snipers and carnivorous insects and tropical snakes that can eat a whole moose in one gulp and earthworms sixteen feet long and then one day when we least expect it this wily sniper'll leap out from behind a blade of grass and powie. Right in the head. [*Serious*] I'm worried.

DICK

Anyone that can spell can get out of Vietnam.

NORMAN

I'm in graduate school. They can't get me.

DICK

Norman, you couldn't buy your way into the army.

NORMAN

I wouldn't go.

MIKE

Why wouldn't you go, Norman?

NORMAN

Huh?

COOTIE

Yeah, think of the army. What about them? They need good graduate students out there in the marshes of Quac Thop Chew Hoy Ben Van Pho Quay Gup Trin.

NORMAN

I don't agree with the war.

MIKE

Well, for God sakes then, let's stop it.

NORMAN

I had my medical and everything. I passed. I could've pretended I was insane or something.

DICK

Pretended?

RUTH

Hey, doesn't anyone here give a shit about Bob.

MIKE

Hey, c'mon, everyone that gives a shit raise your hand.

[COOTIE, MIKE, DICK, *and* NORMAN *raise their hands.*]

See, we all give a shit. So what should we do?

RUTH

Well, I don't know. Maybe we ought to try and find out what's troubling him.

DICK

Maybe he doesn't want us to know. Just maybe.

COOTIE

Yeah, what if he's teetering on the brink of a complete schizophrenic withdrawal and the only thing keeping him sane is knowing we don't know what's troubling him.

MIKE

It's our duty as classmates and favorite turds to leave him alone.

RUTH

Maybe something's wrong between him and Kathy.

DICK

Like what?

RUTH

I don't know. That's what I'm asking.

DICK

He doesn't give a shit about her. Not really. She's just a good lay, that's all.

RUTH

How would you know, Dick?

NORMAN

I thought they were in love.

DICK

Jesus, Norman, where the hell is your head at?

28

NORMAN
Huh?

MIKE
Define the problem, then solve it.

COOTIE
Yeah, what's troubling good old Bob?

MIKE
I think we oughta all go to bed tonight with notebooks under our pillows, and when we get a well-focused and comprehensive idea about the central dilemma of Bob's existence we oughta write it down in clear, concise sentences, with particular attention to grammar and punctuation.

COOTIE
Yeah, then we can meet in here tomorrow and pool our insights.

MIKE
That's a really great plan.

RUTH
I'd really like to know what's troubling him.

DICK
I'd really like to know who the fuck is eating my hamburgers.

NORMAN

Why don't you talk to him?

RUTH

What?

NORMAN

I mean, you know—Bob. If you want to find out what's troubling him, probably the best thing to do is talk to him and say what's troubling you or something like that, and then if he wants to tell you he can and if he doesn't feel like talking about it . . . then . . . well, you know . . .

RUTH

Yeah, maybe I'll do that.

NORMAN

[*Pause*] Yeah, that's what I'd do if I wanted to know. I mean, I'm not saying I wouldn't like to know what's troubling him. I'd really like to know if you find out, but I . . .

[MIKE *has been kneeling by the cat box and peering into it.*]

MIKE

Jesus Christ. Jesus H. fucking Christ.

30

NORMAN
What's wrong?

MIKE
She wasn't even in there.

COOTIE
What! All that time we were looking at an empty box and she wasn't even in there?

MIKE
She must've slipped out while we had our backs turned.

COOTIE
Sneaky little beastie.

MIKE
Cootie, you don't understand. She might be out there in the road right now.

COOTIE
Right now.

MIKE
With all the traffic.

COOTIE
Oh, Christ, and all those architects driving home

drunk from seeing their mistresses . . .

MIKE

And trying to figure out what to tell the little woman. I mean, she's been waiting up all night in a chartreuse quilted sleeping gown with curlers in her hair.

COOTIE

Worrying about the kiddies. Three boys twenty-seven girls. They got appendicitis.

MIKE

Simultaneously. And when she called the kindly family doctor he was away in Cuba . . .

COOTIE

Doing research for his forthcoming book . . .

MIKE

"Chapter Eight: Peritonitis and Social Democracy."

COOTIE

Jesus, I hope we're not too late.

[COOTIE *and* MIKE *rush off down the hall.*]

DICK

Hey, Norman, are these your bananas?

NORMAN
You can have one. I don't mind.

[DICK *takes one and puts the others back in the icebox.*
COOTIE *sticks his head in around the hall door.*]

COOTIE
You coming, Ruth?

RUTH
No.

COOTIE
Your heart is full of bitterness and hate, Ruth.

[COOTIE*'s head disappears again.*]

DICK
You done the essay for Phil 720?

RUTH
No.

DICK
It's due tomorrow.

RUTH
Yeah?

DICK
Yeah.

NORMAN
Is that a good course, Philosophy 720?

RUTH
Nope. Professor Quinn is an albino dwarf queer with halitosis and he smokes too much.

DICK
He does not.

RUTH
Three packs of Pall Mall a day is too much. He's gonna die of cancer.

DICK
He's a genius.

RUTH
You have a thing about queers.

DICK
Fuck off, Ruth.

RUTH
You started it.

[RUTH *goes into hall.* DICK *stands and eats his banana, chewing slowly.* NORMAN *tries to read but* DICK*'s presence distracts him.*]

DICK

How come you're reading that book?

NORMAN

I don't know. It's supposed to be pretty good.

DICK

What are you gonna do when you finish it.

NORMAN

[*Thinks*] I'll start another one.

DICK

Yeah, but what happens when you forget this one. I mean, it'll be as if you hadn't even read it, so what's the point?

NORMAN

Oh, I don't know. I happen to believe you learn things even when you don't know it. Like, if you're reading something right now . . . I mean, I am reading something right now and maybe I'll forget it in a while . . . I mean, I'm forgetting a lot of it already, but I happen to believe I'm being altered in lots of ways I may not be aware of because of . . . well, you know, books and experiences. [*Pause*] Life.

DICK
That's what you believe, huh?

NORMAN
Um, yes, I believe that.

[MIKE *and* COOTIE *enter, wearing heavy winter parkas and boots. They look like trappers.*]

COOTIE
Boy, if we're too late I hate to think of all the dead cats we'll have on our conscience.

MIKE
You gonna help, Dick.

DICK
Fuck off.

MIKE
How about you, Norman, aren't you gonna do your bit for the world of cats?

NORMAN
I'm just in the middle of this chapter.

[MIKE *and* COOTIE *shake their heads in disapproval*

and rush out. NORMAN *tries to read again as* DICK
eats the banana, watching him.]

Hey, it's really hard to read, you know, when someone's
watching you and everything.

DICK

Don't you ever get the feeling you're really irrelevant?

NORMAN

I don't think so.

DICK

[*In one breath*] I mean, you go into the mathematics
department every day and sit there looking out the
window and thinking about cars and women and every
now and then a couple of numbers come into your head
and there's all these Chinese guys running around
solving all the problems worth solving while you sit
there wondering what the hell you're doing.

NORMAN

No, it's not like that. Well, you know, it's not that
simple. I mean . . . [*Pause*] I guess it's a lot like that.
Are you doing anything relevant?

DICK

You can't get more relevant than Far Eastern studies.
Ask me anything about the Far East and I'll tell you the

answer. That's where everything's happening. China, Vietnam, Japan, Korea. You name it.

NORMAN

I guess I ought to know more about those things. I don't know, I keep thinking there's a lot of things I should know about.

DICK

The thing is, Norman, the way I see it, you're already deeply committed to the system. You take away black ghettos, stop the war in Vietnam, distribute the wealth equally throughout the country and you wouldn't be in graduate school.

NORMAN

How come?

DICK

You see, you don't know anything about what makes it all work, do you?

[DICK *throws the banana peel into the cat box.*]

NORMAN

Hey, you shouldn't throw that in there.

DICK

Why not?

NORMAN

Well, I mean, that's the box for the cat. Maybe she won't want to have kittens on a banana peel.

DICK

Norman, how long have you been living here?

NORMAN

Well, you know, about three months. A little longer maybe. About three months and two weeks altogether.

DICK

Have you ever seen a cat around here?

NORMAN

Well, I don't know. I'm out a lot of the time.

DICK

Norman, there is no fucking cat. We haven't got a cat. Boy, for a graduate student you got a lot to learn.

[DICK *starts out but turns to look* NORMAN *over a last time and say . . .*]

Jesus.

[*Then he's gone down the hall.* NORMAN *kneels by the cat box and examines it as some muffled piano chords fill the silence. It's* BOB *playing a lazy, rich, drifting progression, moody-Bill-Evans-style.* KATHY *walks through the kitchen in a man's robe carrying a towel. She lights the stack heater. From inside the hall we hear* DICK*'s voice yelling.*]

DICK

STOP PLAYING THAT FUCKING NOISE. I'M TRYING TO READ. HEY, BOB.

[KATHY *goes to the hall door and yells down.*]

KATHY

Mind your own goddamn business, Richard.

[*A door slams, and the music, which had stopped momentarily, starts again, but louder.*]

[*Turning*] Hey listen, Norman. If you're gonna be in here for a while could you do me a favor and make sure no one turns off the water heater, 'cause I'm just taking a shower. And if you get a chance could you put on some coffee, 'cause I'll be coming out in about ten minutes and I'd like a cup when I come out. OK?

NORMAN

Do you have any books on Vietnam?

KATHY

[*Pause*] Yeah. A few.

NORMAN
Are they good books?

KATHY
Well, you know, some are, some aren't. Why?

NORMAN
I just, you know, wondered, that's all.

[KATHY *watches* NORMAN *go to the stove and fumble around with the coffee percolator. She shrugs and goes out. We hear the bathroom door close and, moments later, the sound of a shower running.*]

Actually, I've been thinking I'd like to read some books about Vietnam. I mean it's been going on all this time. I don't know, though. I've never read any books about it. Maybe if I could read one book, then I'd know a little more about it and I could decide if I wanted to read another. Would it be OK if I borrowed one of your books to start with? I'd give it back as soon as I finished it.

[*He looks around and sees he's alone. He goes out the door. We hear the bathroom door opening and a yell.*]

KATHY
Goddamnit, Norman, what are you doing in here?

NORMAN

I was wondering if you'd lend me . . .

KATHY

Hey, get the hell out of here, I'm taking a shower.

   [*A door slams.*]

NORMAN

I just wanted to know if it was OK for me to borrow one of those books about Vietnam.

KATHY

Well, Jesus Christ, can't you wait till I'm done?

NORMAN

Oh . . . yeah, I'm sorry. [*Pause*] Is that all right with you?

KATHY

Hey, don't stand around out there. You can borrow as many goddamn books as you want, only get away from the door, 'cause it just so happens I don't like a lot of people standing around outside the bathroom door while I'm washing.

   [NORMAN *comes back into the kitchen. He fixes a little more of the coffee, then goes to the hall door and yells down the hallway.*]

NORMAN

I'll just make the coffee first, and when you're finished in there I'll come down to your room with you and get the book. Hey, listen, if you decide to have your coffee in here, could you go down to your room first and bring the book in with you? Yes, that's probably better. Hey, is that OK? [*Pause*] Hey, is that OK?

[*No answer.* NORMAN *is left baffled, as the lights dim and* BOB's *piano chords keep going and going.*]

End of scene 1

ℰscene 2

[*It's a few days later.* NORMAN *is reading,* RUTH *is making sandwiches, and* COOTIE *and* MIKE *are rolling up a banner.*]

COOTIE

I don't know about the wording.

MIKE

I think it's pretty good wording.

COOTIE

I'm not too happy about it.

MIKE

You're unhappy about the wording.

COOTIE

Well, I'm not, you know, cut up about it or anything, but I'm definitely not as happy as I could be about it.

MIKE

Ruthie, we need an impartial third voice over here.

RUTH

Who wants orange marmalade?

MIKE

I'd like an orange marmalade.

COOTIE

I want two orange marmalade and one chunky peanut butter, please.

RUTH

How 'bout you, Norman?

COOTIE

And I wouldn't mind a chunky peanut butter and orange marmalade mixed.

RUTH

Hey, Norman, do you want sandwiches or not?

COOTIE

You gotta have sandwiches handy if you're coming, Norman. On your average march you'll find you get through a good two peanut butter and jellies before you even get to where you're supposed to demonstrate, and then after circling round and yelling militant slogans at the monument or park or poison gas plant or nuclear missile establishment for a couple hours, you're just about ready for another peanut butter and jelly.

MIKE

Or cream cheese and olives.

COOTIE

Bacon, lettuce, and tomato. I mean, I know you meet a lotta pretty groovy people at these marches, but you can't count on them having extra sandwiches for a new acquaintance.

RUTH

Hey, Norman, willya please tell me if you're coming with us or not?

NORMAN

[*Unfriendly*] I'm going with Dick.

COOTIE

You're lucky there. You'll get hamburger on toasted roll if you go with Dick. He takes sterno and cooks right out there in the middle of lines of charging cops and tear gas and mace and everything.

[DICK *enters.*]

MIKE

Hey, Dick, you better hurry up and get dressed for the march.

COOTIE

Yeah, Dick, you don't want to be late or all the best ass'll be grabbed up.

DICK

[*Indicating banner*] What's it say?

COOTIE

"Buy Government bonds."

MIKE

"Plant an avocado today and have a fruit-bearing tree in six years."

RUTH

You want some of our peanut butter and marmalade?

MIKE

What's this about giving away all our peanut butter and marmalade all of a sudden? He wouldn't give us any of his lousy hamburgers. We had to pay for those hamburgers on common stock.

DICK

Where's Kathy and Bob?

47

MIKE

Yeah, where's good old Bob? [*Yells*] HEY, YOU GUYS ARE YOU COMING?

KATHY

[*Inside*] Yeah, hold on a minute, willya?

MIKE

They're coming.

COOTIE

Hey, Norman, I been watching you pretty closely for the last few days and I have this definite impression you've been displaying hostility toward me, Mike, and Ruth, in that order.

NORMAN

I'm just reading this book . . .

COOTIE

Don't be negative, Norman. You're trying to pretend I hadn't noticed your emotions. You happen to be up against a disciple of Freud, Jung, Adler, Pavlov, Skinner, and the honorable L. Ron Hubbard, to mention but a few. It just so happens I can detect subatomic trace particles of hostility within a six-mile radius of anywhere I am.

MIKE

It's no use contradicting him, Norman. If he says he can

feel hostility, that's it. I mean, even I can feel it and I'm only moderately sensitive to hostility up to about a hundred eighty yards.

NORMAN
I'm not feeling hostile . . .

COOTIE
You're not only feeling it, you're dying to tell us about it. That's a basic axiom of hostility.

NORMAN
Oh, boy, you guys.

DICK
Leave him alone.

COOTIE
Dick, that's the worst thing you can do. I know you think you're being a good shit and everything, but if the guy is riddled with hostility and he doesn't get it out of his system it's gonna go haywire and zing all around inside his body till he's twenty-eight years old and then he'll get cancer.

RUTH
You know, we're gonna be really late if those guys don't hurry up . . .

MIKE
That reminds me of a guy I was reading about. He got

49

so pent up with hostility his head fell right down inside his body, no shit, that's what I was reading, right down between his shoulders.

COOTIE
Fell?

MIKE
Yeah, straight down till all you could see was these two little eyeballs peering out over his collarbone.

COOTIE
Mike.

MIKE
What, Mel?

COOTIE
[*Pause*] Fell?

MIKE
[*Pause*] Sank?

COOTIE
Subsided.

MIKE
Right.

COOTIE

In fact, as I remember it, his head eventually disappeared completely.

MIKE

Don't rush me, I'm coming to that. Now, Norman, I want you to pay very close attention because this case is a lesson in itself. You see, everybody used to warn this particular guy to loosen up and maybe see an analyst, but the guy refused on the grounds that it would cost too much, and that turned out to be really stupid economy, because with his head inside him like that he couldn't see anything and he had to hire a guy, full time, seven days a week, to lead him around. The guy was so tight with his money he tried to solve the problem by rigging up this ingenious system of mirrors, like a periscope, but the natural movements of his body kept knocking the mirrors out of alignment, so in addition to the guy that led him around, he had to hire another guy, full time, seven days a week, to keep readjusting the mirrors. You can imagine the expense involved.

COOTIE

There was a very fine article about that guy in the *Hostility Journal*, spring number. Did you happen to catch that article, Norman?

NORMAN

I'm not listening.

MIKE

Did it tell about what happened to him?

COOTIE

Well, it was one of those stories in two parts, and wouldn't you know it, that's just when my subscription ran out.

MIKE

Oh well, you missed the best part. You see, when his head got down as f . . . subsided as far as his stomach . . .

COOTIE

. . . thank you . . .

MIKE

. . . he went and hired a top-notch transplant surgeon to replace his belly button with a flexible, clear plastic window so he could see where he was going.

COOTIE

Jumpin' Jehoshaphat!

MIKE

And I'm happy to announce, the operation was a complete success.

COOTIE

Fantastic! No problems with rejection or anything?

MIKE

Nope. The Dow Chemical Company set up a ten-man, two-woman research team and they developed a type of clear plastic window that matched the guy's antibodies perfectly. In a matter of weeks, the guy was able to live a completely normal life again, skin diving, stamp collecting, a lot of political work. He could even go to the movies when he felt like it, but he had to sit up on the back of the seat and it caused a lot of hard feelings with the people sitting directly behind him. But that's the great thing about the average movie-going audience; they respected his infirmity.

COOTIE

Fuck a duck!

MIKE

Shut up, sonny boy, I ain't finished yet.

COOTIE

There's more?

MIKE

Yeah, you see, the really incredible thing was when the guy woke up one morning and realized his head was still sinking . . .

COOTIE

. . . subsiding . . .

53

MIKE

. . . and he went to this doctor to check it out. He was just walking along, you know, and when he got to this corner to stop for a red light a dog peed on his leg, and when he bent forward to see what was making his pants wet a guy up on some scaffolding right behind dropped a pipe wrench on his back, and the impact of this wrench, plus the slightly inclined position of the guy's upper body, knocked his head back into place.

COOTIE

Hot diggity!

MIKE

Well, the guy went apeshit, jumping all over the place, singing songs right out there on the streets . . . and that's just when it all had to happen. This poor guy, after all his suffering, was finally looking forward to a happy and productive life . . .

COOTIE

Oh, shit, yeah, I remember now. The poor son of a bitch.

MIKE

Yeah, you 'member, he was just standing out there in the street stopping traffic in both directions, tears of humble gratitude streaming down his cheeks and some stupid . . .

54

[*He sees* KATHY *and* BOB *standing in the hallway door ready for the march.*]

. . . oh, hi, Bob, hi, Kathy.

RUTH

Hey, do you guys want some of our peanut butter and marmalade?

BOB

I've got an announcement.

COOTIE

We used to have a nearsighted canary . . .

RUTH

Listen, I gotta make these sandwiches and we're gonna end up short if I don't get some cooperation around here.

COOTIE

Hey, Norman hasn't even got a banner. Norman, aren't you gonna bring a banner?

BOB

Mel, willya please shut up. I'm trying to tell you guys something?

COOTIE

Well, fuck you, I'm talking to Norman. You want him to get all the way down to the demonstration and they disqualify him 'cause he doesn't have a banner.

RUTH

Everyone is gonna fucking well eat whatever I make.

DICK

You want some help.

RUTH

Look, it's not like I don't know how to make sandwiches . . .

MIKE

Hey, everyone, c'mon, c'mon, let's have a little order around here. Everybody stay where you are and don't panic. OK, Bob, I think we got everything under control now.

BOB

Thank you.

MIKE

That's OK, Bob.

BOB

I've just got this . . .

MIKE
Bob?

BOB
What?

MIKE
Anytime.

BOB
What?

MIKE
Anytime you want a little peace and quiet so you can
make an announcement without a lot of people talking
over you, just ask me and I'll do what I can for you.

BOB
Thank you, Mike.

MIKE
That's OK, Bob, you're a good shit.

[BOB *hesitates, trying to find words to frame his vague
thoughts. When he speaks, it is halting . . .*]

BOB
Look . . . I just thought maybe it was about time
somebody around here . . .

MIKE

Do you want some water or anything?

RUTH

Oh for chrissake, shut up, Mike.

COOTIE

[*Cooling things*] Yeah, shut yer mouth, sonny boy, yer creatin' a public nuisance.

RUTH

Go on, Bob.

BOB

No, no, look, all I want to say is . . . Norman, if there is one way to remain irrelevant and ineffective it's to sit with your nose buried in a book while life is raging all around you.

[NORMAN *looks up and closes his book.*]

Thank you. OK. Announcement . . .

[BOB *walks around the room, again trying to think of how to put it. As he starts to speak . . .*]

MIKE

Earthquakes in Singapore . . . ?

58

RUTH
[*Incredible rage*] SHUT UP!

BOB
Never mind.

MIKE
Sorry. I'm sorry.

KATHY
What's wrong, Bob?

BOB
Really, nothing, nothing at all. I just had this stupid
thought the other day in humanities. Johnson was
saying something idiotic, as usual, and I just started to
watch him carefully for the first time talking to us, you
know, thirty kids who think he's a prick, and I realized
that he probably thinks all of us are pricks . . . and I
just started to wonder what the fuck we're all doing.
You know what I mean? What the fuck are we all
doing, seriously, tell me, I'd really like to know . . . in
twenty-five words or less. . . . No, no, sorry, come on,
carnival time. Let's go marching.

KATHY
I found the letter, Bob.

BOB
What letter?

[KATHY *takes an official letter out of her bag.*]

Kathy, where the hell did you get that? Come on, give it here.

KATHY

We're supposed to be like all together in here. If you can't say it yourself, I'll say it for you.

[BOB *is momentarily confused, then realizes that* KATHY *thinks he was trying to tell everyone about the letter. He finds the situation absurd, annoying, and funny.*]

BOB

Kathy, that letter has nothing to do with anything and it's none of your business and would you please give it back.

[KATHY *hands the letter to* RUTH. RUTH *reads.*]

RUTH

Oh, fuck.

[RUTH *hands the letter on. Each reads in turn. It ends in* MIKE*'s hands.* BOB *waits impatiently as the letter makes its round. He's embarrassed and then begins to find it funny that everyone, especially* KATHY, *has construed the letter as his problem.* MIKE *is by now looking quite seriously at him.*]

BOB

[*Laughing it off*] It's just for the physical. I mean, I'm not dead yet.

[*As* BOB *says this, something amusing passes through his mind and he stops talking. He turns the thought over in his mind.* MIKE *is looking at the letter again. The others watch* BOB.]

MIKE

They misspelled your name?

[BOB *comes out of his brief daydream.*]

BOB

Huh?

MIKE

Jobert.

BOB

[*Amused*] Oh, yeah.

MIKE

Jobert Rettie. Dear Jobert Rettie. Hi, Jobert.

BOB

Hi, Jike.

MIKE

Good old Jobert.

COOTIE
How ya feelin', good old Jobert?

BOB
Dead, how 'bout you?

[MIKE *sees what's happening and comes to the rescue.*]

MIKE
[*Pause*] Hi, Jel.

COOTIE
Hi, Jike.

MIKE
Hi, Jorman.

NORMAN
Huh?

MIKE
Hi, Jorman.

NORMAN
Oh, hi.

MIKE
Hi, Jathy, hi, Jick.

62

DICK

Fuck off.

MIKE

Juck off? Why should I juck off, Jick?

[*The doorbell rings.* COOTIE *rushes over and answers it. At the door, a young man in a suit and tie and horn-rimmed glasses, with an attaché case, which he has concealed just out of sight behind the doorframe.*]

COOTIE

Hi, Jister.

MIKE

Ask him his name, Jel.

COOTIE

What's your name?

RALPH

Ralph.

COOTIE

Hi Jalph, I'm Jel and that's Jathy, Jorman, Jike, Jick, and Job, and we're just on our way down to City Hall to beat the shit out of some cops. Wanna come?

[RALPH *pauses momentarily, then launches his pitch.*]

RALPH

I'm from the University of Buffalo and I'm in the neighborhood doing market research. You don't mind my asking you a few questions, do you?

[*As he says this last, he reaches down, takes up his concealed attaché case, bends his head down, like making ready for a dive, and advances swiftly but deliberately into the middle of the room. This swift movement, plus the running patter, is designed to force the average housewife to back away and give ground, but since* COOTIE *merely steps aside when* RALPH *bends down for his attaché case, we are treated to the entire technique out of context.* RALPH *ends up in the middle of the room, still bent over, motionless. He looks up and around and straightens himself, laughing nervously at everyone watching him.*]

Do all you people live here?

MIKE

No, we're just using the place for a few days. This is a fantastic coincidence because the guy that lives here just went away for a few days to do a series of special guest lectures at the University of Buffalo.

RALPH

Really? No kidding? That's some coincidence, huh? That's really a fantastic coincidence. Well, ahhh, here's what I'd like to do. I'd like to interview one of you people. I'll choose one of you at random and everybody else can listen and if the guy I choose has a particular opinion that differs significantly from what the rest of you believe, we'll just stop and take a consensus, OK? Hey, you guys all work, don't you? I mean, you're not students or anything?

COOTIE

We mostly hold various government jobs.

RALPH

I see. Are any of you married?

RUTH

I'm married to him [MIKE] and she's married to him [BOB *and* KATHY].

BOB

Actually, we're getting a divorce.

RALPH

Oh, I'm very sorry.

BOB

[*Very sincerely to* RALPH] No, please. It's just, I've been dying for a while, nothing serious, you know, but now I've decided I'm definitely dead, you see, so I'll have to change my name. It's a legal technicality. We'll marry again under my new name. Jobert. [*Pause*] Job.

RALPH

Oh . . . well . . . that's certainly very unusual. Now this is going to get a little difficult, really. I've got to improvise some of these questions because the standard form is pretty rigid, like, you know, it asks things about your children's opinions and that would hardly apply in a case like . . .

MIKE

I have several kids by a former marriage.

RUTH

Hey, how come you never told me about that?

MIKE

If you remember, dear, we did discuss it.

RALPH

Can I just edge in here, I mean, ha-ha, I don't want to interrupt a little marital tiff or anything, but, ha-ha, you know. [*To* NORMAN] And how about you, sir, do you have any children?

NORMAN

I don't have any children. I'm not married.

RALPH

Well, sir, I would guess, am I right, I would guess that you are the oldest person staying here. I only mean that in the sense of responsibility. Am I right?

MIKE

The guy that actually lives here is older, but he's not here right now.

RALPH

No, he's lecturing, right? I remember, ha-ha. Now I'd just like to ask you the following question. Have you ever heard of a teaching program called the World Volumes Encyclopedia?

DICK

Hey, are you selling encyclopedias?

RUTH

Hey, yeah, are you trying to sell us a set of encyclopedias?

RALPH

I'd like to make it very clear that I am not authorized to sell any product, I'm merely doing market research.

MIKE

Jesus Christ, he's not even selling the fucking things. You go and write to the central offices and you wait for a whole year to hear from them and when they finally decide to send a guy around he's not even authorized to sell you a set. I'm not hanging around here listening to a guy that isn't even authorized to sell the World Volumes Encyclopedia while millions of women and children are dying out there in Vietnam.

[MIKE *grabs the banner and starts huzzahing as everyone follows him out of the door.* DICK *and* NORMAN *stay behind with* RALPH, *who is yelling after them.*]

RALPH
Hey, hey, listen, I can sell you a set if you want one.

[RALPH *turns to* DICK *and* NORMAN.]

Hey, do you guys really want to buy a set of encyclopedias? I can sell you a set. I got a number of deals and there's a special discount for government employees.

DICK
[*To* NORMAN] You going?

NORMAN
Yes, I've been reading a lot about it lately.

DICK

You want to come with me?

NORMAN

Well, yeah, if you don't have any other plans.

DICK

OK, hold on a minute.

[DICK *goes out the hall door.*]

RALPH

Hey, who are all you people?

NORMAN

We just live here.

RALPH

I go to college. I don't really come from Buffalo. I live in town. I'm trying to earn some money in my spare time. Are you guys really government employees?

NORMAN

I'm a graduate student.

RALPH

Yeah, well, I didn't want to say anything, but I didn't

really think you guys were government employees. What are you studying?

NORMAN
Mathematics.

RALPH
I wanted to study mathematics. My father said he wouldn't pay so I'm studying law. Boy, do I hate law. I'm living at home. Do you guys all live here together?

NORMAN
Yes.

RALPH
And . . . and the girls too?

NORMAN
Yes.

RALPH
Oh boy, what a life, huh? I'm gonna get me a car pretty soon. I'm saving up. The thing is, I'm not really doing too well selling encyclopedias. I can't pull it off. I wish I could figure out why. I've been thinking about it and I think maybe it's because I can't give the sales pitch

credibility. That's pretty bad if I'm gonna be a lawyer because a lot of the time you have to defend people you know are guilty. The thing is, these encyclopedias are really shitty. [*He blushes*] Sorry. I mean, you know, they're not very good.

[DICK *reenters. He is carefully groomed and well dressed in a pea jacket and well-laundered jeans. He wears a large, orange Dayglo peace button.*]

DICK
You ready?

RALPH
You going out?

DICK
Listen, if you're gonna eat anything, lay off the hamburgers OK?

[DICK *and* NORMAN *start out.*]

NORMAN
I don't see why he has to go saying he's dead. I mean, that's only for him to have a physical. It's pretty easy to fail a physical. I've heard of guys that pretend . . .

[*They are gone.* RALPH, *alone, looks at the open door.*]

RALPH
Hey!

[*Blackout.*]

End of scene 2

scene 3

[*A few hours later.* KATHY *is sitting in the kitchen, crying.* RUTH *comes in the front door. She has just returned from the march.*]

RUTH
Bob here?

KATHY
No.

RUTH
Hey, what's wrong. You want some coffee?

KATHY
Please.

[RUTH *takes off her coat and starts making coffee.*]

How was it?

RUTH

Weren't you there?

KATHY

No.

RUTH

I thought you and Bob were coming. You were on the bus and everything. I got lost when the cops charged. Boy, they really got some of those guys. Fucking pigs.

KATHY

When we got there he said he didn't feel like marching.

RUTH

Why not?

KATHY

Oh, Ruthie, I don't know. I don't know anything any more. You devote two years to a guy and what does he give you? He never even told me about that letter. Drafted, and he didn't even tell me.

RUTH

He's not drafted. That letter's for the physical. All he has to do is act queer. They're not gonna take a queer musician.

KATHY

That's what I told him on the bus. He wouldn't even listen until I called him Job.

RUTH

What?

KATHY

He said he was dead. "Bob is dead."

RUTH

Bullshit, he's putting you on.

KATHY

That's what I mean. Me. He's even putting me on. Ungrateful bastard. The things I've done for him, Ruthie. Shit, I sound just like my mother. You know what I mean. I'm not complaining, but you know, you get tired of giving all the time and nothing's coming back. You know what I told him? I said he was the first guy I ever had an orgasm with. I mean, it really made him feel good. Now I gotta live with it. How can you explain something like that?

RUTH

Hey, no shitting around, did he really say he was gonna join?

KATHY

Ruthie, I'm telling you, he's serious. You know what he told me? He thinks the whole antiwar movement is a goddamn farce. I mean, Jesus, I really thought we were relating on that one. It's not like I'm asking the guy to go burn himself or anything but, I mean, he knows how I feel about the war and he's just doing it to be shitty. There's something behind it, I know that. He's like reaching out, trying to relate to me on the personal level by rejecting me but, like, I don't know how to break through. He says he's gonna study engineering in the army and then when he gets out he's gonna get some kind of plastic job and marry a plastic wife and live in a plastic house in some fucking plastic suburb and have two point seven children. Oh shit, Ruth, it's all too much. He went to a cowboy film.

RUTH

Well, you know, that's how it is.

KATHY

But Ruth, it's not like a fantasy scene. I know the guy. He'll go through with it. I mean, he really thinks he's serious. He doesn't see it's all part of a communication thing between him and me.

RUTH

I don't know. Like, maybe he's really serious. Mike's got this thing about physics. His tutor says he's a genius.

OK, maybe he is, like what do I know about physics?
The thing is, he's gonna end up working for his old man
in the lumber business. It's all laid out from the start.
You have to fit in.

KATHY

You don't want him to do that, do you? If the guy is
into physics you've gotta really stand behind him and
make it all happen for him.

RUTH

I don't know. You have some kids and everything. I
mean it's not like you can't have a meaningful life if you
get married and have kids.

KATHY

Wow, I don't believe you really mean that.

RUTH

Look, Kathy, I don't want Mike to saw wood for the
rest of his life, but what can I do about it? Why
shouldn't he get into wood? Like, what if he does
physics for the rest of his life and he's a genius and ends
up head of department at some asshole university? You
find out one day he's being financed by the C.I.A.

KATHY

These guys. They think they don't need you, so you go
away and they freak out. Mike is a really brilliant guy. I

mean, we all know that. You could really do things for him if you tried. You should've seen Bob when I first met him.

RUTH
I did.

KATHY
He used to compose all this really shitty music and like when he did something good he didn't even know it. You had to keep telling him yes, it's good, it's really great. A whole year it took for him to believe it. He's writing some fantastic stuff now, ever since, you know, I told him he was the first guy.

RUTH
Yeah, and look at him now.

KATHY
[*Crying again*] You think you're really relating like crazy and then, I don't know, it's a whole new scene. It's like you don't even know him any more.

RUTH
Maybe you ought to stop relating so hard.

KATHY
You don't know him, Ruth. I really know the guy and he needs me.

RUTH

Yeah, but maybe you ought to lay off for a while.

[MIKE *bursts in through the front door.*]

MIKE

Holy shit, where were you?

RUTH

I got lost and came home.

MIKE

Christ, it was horrible. We got stopped by this line of cops. Me and Cootie were right up front so I told him we should get everyone to join hands and stand still. We're standing there and this one pig starts running toward Cootie and you know how he gets when he sees pigs and he always gets diarrhea. I don't know, he should have said something, but he got the urge so bad he started to run, you know, trying to find a toilet, and this dumb pig thought he was trying to resist arrest.

KATHY

Is he all right?

MIKE

They took him to the hospital. He's, I don't know, they said he'll be all right. He got it in the back.

[COOTIE *walks in.*]

COOTIE

Boy, what a shitty march. You had to go and get separated with all the eats. I could've really used a marmalade and chunky peanut butter.

RUTH

Hey, did you know, Bob really wants to join the army. He's not even gonna try and get out. He didn't even go to the march.

COOTIE

He didn't miss much.

KATHY

He went to a goddamn cowboy film.

COOTIE

Hey, is that the one with Kirk Douglas and Gina Lollobrigida and Curt Jurgens and Orson Welles and Tom Courtenay and . . .

KATHY

You guys are really something. You don't give a shit what happens to him. I thought we were, like, all together here. Smug bastards. I'll tell you something.

COOTIE

What's that, Kathy.

KATHY

You're no better than the people fighting this war.

[KATHY *storms out of the room down the hall.*]

MIKE

She's pretty cut up, huh?

RUTH

She thinks he's serious.

MIKE

Isn't he?

[COOTIE *starts jumping and singing, punctuating each note with a leap. He snarls the song.*]

COOTIE

We shall overcu—u—um,
We shall overcu—u—um,
We shall overcome some day—ay–ay–ay–ay
Oh, oh, oh, deep in my heart
I do believe.
We shall over . . .

MIKE

Shut up, Mel.

81

COOTIE

If Bob's really serious, we gotta stop the war quick so he doesn't get sent over there to get killed by an antipersonnel bullet.

[DICK *comes in, livid.*]

DICK

Fucking Norman is fucking out of his fucking mind. That's the last time I ever take him with me.

[DICK *takes a bottle of milk from the icebox, kills it, and places it on the stack.*]

MIKE

Hey, what's the matter, Dick, didn't you get yourself some left-wing ass?

COOTIE

Don't be ashamed, sonny. If she's waiting out there in the hallway, bring her in and show us the goods.

DICK

Norman had a fucking gun with him. He took a fucking revolver to the march.

MIKE

Is he a good shot?

DICK

I'm not shitting around. We're sitting on the bus and he's telling me he's reading Ho Chi Minh on guerrilla war and he doesn't think marches are effective. So he says he's gonna use the marchers like an indigenous population and start a guerrilla war against the cops. I mean, I thought he was just fucking around. You know Norman. Then he pulls out this fucking revolver right there on the bus, people looking and everything, and he says he's gonna get a few cops and would I help him create a diversion. He's out of his fucking mind.

MIKE

How many'd he get?

DICK

Fuck you.

COOTIE

He got the girl, huh?

DICK

Where's Kathy and Bob?

RUTH

Bob's not here.

DICK

Kathy here?

RUTH

Leave her alone. She's upset.

COOTIE

Yeah, I wouldn't try to lay her just yet, 'cause she's still going with Bob.

[DICK *walks out down the hall.*]

MIKE

That was a pretty stupid thing to say.

COOTIE

Just came out.

RUTH

Who cares? Everyone knows what dirty Dicky's up to. Except maybe Bob.

MIKE

And maybe Kathy.

RUTH

Kathy knows.

COOTIE

Do you think a guy could become a homosexual just by willpower? Could someone learn to like guys?

[*A knock on the front door.*]

RUTH

It's open.

[*In walks* LUCKY, *the downstairs neighbor, led by* MR.
WILLIS, *the landlord.*]

WILLIS

Lucky tells me there's been a lotta noise up here. Is that
right?

MIKE

Sorry, Mr. Willis, we had a little outburst up here. It's
my fault. I just got a letter my sister had a baby.

COOTIE

We were celebrating.

WILLIS

That's all right, but keep it down. Lucky here was
saying how you woke his wife up. She's a very ill
person. I don't want any more complaints.

MIKE

Don't you worry about that, Mr. Willis, I'll take it on
myself to keep this place really quiet.

LUCKY

Listen, I told you kids once before, and I'm not telling
you again. You gotta get rid of those galvanized

aluminum garbage cans in the yard and get plastic ones like everyone else.

RUTH

Listen, I don't see why we can't keep the ones . . .

MIKE

Ruth, now calm down, Ruth. I'm sorry, Lucky, but Ruth's pretty upset. Her father's fallen ill and they don't know for sure if it's . . . you know.

LUCKY

You got the galvanized aluminum out there. You'll have to get rid of the galvanized aluminum ones and get plastic.

WILLIS

I'll take care of the rest, Lucky. Thank you for bringing this particular grievance to my attention.

LUCKY

I'll give you till Monday, then I want to see plastic out there.

[LUCKY *leaves through front door.*]

WILLIS

Whew, I hope I seen the last of that loony today. Nothin' but complaints day and night. The guy was born with a hair across his ass. So who's gonna give the landlord a little coffee?

[RUTH *makes a move to get it.*]

Thanks, sweetheart. Brother, what a day, what a stinker of a day. Where's Bobby?

MIKE
He's dead.

WILLIS
Dead? He's dead? You guys really kill me, you guys. You got a whole sense of humor like nothin' else. Dead, huh? Smart kid, Bobbie. Hey, you been to the march?

COOTIE
Yep.

WILLIS
Great march. I watched it on Channel 8 in color. Brother, clothes you guys wear come out really good on color TV. You know, that guy Lucky can be a lotta trouble. He got a mind, like, you know, the size of a pinhead, you know what I mean? Just one sugar, sweetheart.

MIKE
You want the rent?

WILLIS

Rent, schment. I come to see how you guys are getting
along and you talk to me about rent. How many
landlords care, tell me that? One in a million, I can
tellya. Hey, you decided whatya gonna do when you get
out of college?

COOTIE

I'm gonna be a homosexual.

WILLIS

A homo. . . . You guys really slay me, you guys. What
a sense of humor. You know, I'd give ten'a my other
tenants for any one of you guys. You kids are the future
of America, I mean that deeply, not too much milk,
beautiful. Yeah, you kids live a great life up here. I got
tenants complaining all the time about the way you kids
carry on, and I'll tell ya something, you wanna know
why they complain? 'Cause they'd give the last piece of
hair on their heads to live like you kids are living.

RUTH

How's Mrs. Willis?

WILLIS

Huh? Oh, yeah, great, just great. Well, just between you
and me and the wall she's gettin' to be a pain in the ass.
She wants me to get rid of you, too. Why? I ask her.
She don't like the way you live. OK, I say, if you know

so much, how do they live? She don't know and she don't wanna know. I try to tell her, you know, about the wild parties and stuff and taking drugs to have all new sensations in the body and the orgies with six or seven of you all at once. You should see her eyes light up. Same thing with all the tenants. When they hear what it's really like up here they go all funny. They'd pay me a hunnerd dollars to hear more, but they ain't got the nerve to ask. Get rid of them. That's all I hear. Wamme to tell you something?

MIKE

If you got something to say you didn't ought to hold back.

WILLIS

Tremendous. You kids are tremendous. Listen. When the neighbors try to tellya about when they was young, don't believe it. It's a lotta bull, and I should know. When we was young it was so boring you fell asleep when you was twenty and you never woke up again. You hear them stories Lucky tells about the war. Crap. He's sittin' down there holdin' his dink and watchin' Doris Day on television. He'd give his left nut to know what's happenin' up here. This is the best cup of coffee I've had all day. I got a theory about it. It's when the head and the stomach don't talk to each other no more. That's when everything goes to hell. I'm gettin' so I don't know what I want half the time. I got these dreams, really crazy dreams. I got this one where I'm in a clearing, you know, it's right in the middle of the jungle and there's this tribe of Africans, I mean, like I don't know if they're Africans but they're livin' in the jungle and they're black so I figure they must be Africans. They got this skin, it's, you know, black, but really black. This maybe sounds kind of screwy but it's really beautiful, this skin. It's a dream, remember. I'm not sayin' black skin is beautiful, if you see what I mean. I'm in charge of the whole works in this jungle and I got it all organized so the men live in one hut and the women live in another hut and there's a big sort of square in between where nobody's allowed after lights-out. They live like this all their life. There's no marryin' or anything. I'm a kind of witch doctor and I got this tribe believing . . . well, you know, they're just, like, Africans, and they don't know you gotta have a man and a woman to make babies, and I got 'em thinkin' you get babies when the moon shines down a girl's cunt and hits the inside of her womb. And I got this whole ceremony where a girl comes to me when she wants a baby and I tell her she gotta wait until it gets dark and the moon comes up. Then I tie her to a plank, face up, and tilt the plank so her thing is facing the moon and then I go to the hut with the guys inside and get one of them to jerk off on a leaf, you know, one of them tropical leafs that's really big. Then I roll this leaf up like it's a tube and I sneak across the square holding this leaf in my hand, all rolled up, until I get to the girl. She's lying there in the moonlight all black and shiny

and her thing is opened right up 'cause she thinks . . .
and I got this tube full of jis in my hand, and I'm
coming closer so I can smell everything and . . . [*Comes
out of it*] Jesus, what am I saying? I'm going crazy. It's
just a dream, what I'm telling you.

RUTH
That's the most beautiful thing I ever heard.

WILLIS
Listen, I got carried away. I didn't mean none of that.

MIKE
Mr. Willis, if you'd've had the opportunities we've had
you'd've probably ended up one of the great poets of the
century, and I mean that includes Rimbaud, Rilke,
Williams, Pasternak, and Ginsberg.

COOTIE
And Whitman.

MIKE
Yes, Whitman included.

WILLIS
Oh Jesus, you kids, you kids. I feel like I can tell you
anything. Somebody could've thought I was pretty
screwy if I told them some of them things.

RUTH

How many landlords have poetry in their soul?

WILLIS

Yeah, yeah. Hey, I gotta run now. Listen, it's really great having you guys around. If I could get some of them other tenants to come up here and listen to you the world would be a better place to live in, you know what I mean?

MIKE

It would be a much better place.

COOTIE

A hundred percent better, at least.

RUTH

You're a beautiful person, Mr. Willis. Never be ashamed of it.

WILLIS

No, I ain't. I ain't ashamed of myself. Hey, you know what I was sayin' before about all them complaints. I lost a lotta tenants on account of you. I can't afford any more, so keep it quiet or I'll have to get rid of you. Wonderful coffee, sweetheart. Seeya.

[WILLIS *leaves through front door.*]

RUTH

I wonder how long before they put him away?

[KATHY, *clothes a bit messed up, flounces into the kitchen and gets a glass of water.* DICK *follows her as far as the kitchen, as if he was trying to stop her, but when he gets to the doorframe he stops, feeling the tension in the room. He tries to button his shirt casually, not sure whether he wants the others to know what just happened between him and* KATHY.]

COOTIE

Hi, Dick, how's it hanging?

[KATHY *stiffens at the sink.* DICK *turns and goes down the hall out of sight.*]

MIKE

I still can't figure out what to get good old Bob for Christmas.

[*Before* KATHY *can reply, the doorbell rings. No one moves.*]

COOTIE

Whose turn is it?

KATHY

You're a miserable bastard.

COOTIE

What'd I say? We're just playing a chess tournament.

KATHY

Listen, this is my scene, mine. You guys stay out of it,
OK, Ruth!

RUTH

It's her scene, guys, you stay out of it.

COOTIE

Roger.

MIKE

Sam.

COOTIE

Larry.

MIKE

Richard.

COOTIE

What's Richard getting Bob for Christmas?

[*The doorbell rings again, and* MIKE *jumps up to get
it.* SHELLY*'s standing there.*]

MIKE

Hello there, I don't know you.

SHELLY

Hi. Does Norman live here?

MIKE

Does anyone here know a Norman?

SHELLY

He said he lived here. I met him at the march today. He said to come here and wait for him. I been standing out in the hall 'cause, like, I heard someone talking and I didn't want to disturb anyone and then this guy just came out so I figured, well, it's now or never kind of thing. I'm Shelly.

RUTH

Come on in. I'm Ruth.

SHELLY

Oh, good, then Norman does live here because I wasn't sure when he gave me the address. Sometimes you meet a guy at a march and he'll like give you an address and you end up waiting for a few days and he never shows. Did that ever happen to you? It's happened to me a lot of times.

KATHY

Listen, everyone, I'm serious, I don't want him to know. I'll tell him when the time's right.

RUTH

It's your scene.

[KATHY *exits down hall.* SHELLY, *meanwhile, goes under the table and sits down on the floor.*]

SHELLY

I'm sorry about this. If you want to laugh go ahead. I'm used to it. It's just I've got this thing at the moment where I keep sitting under tables and I figured I'd better do it right away instead of pretending for a while I didn't sit under tables. I mean, sitting under the table is "me" at the moment, so why hide it? Have you ever done it?

RUTH

Want some coffee, Shelly?

SHELLY

I'm a vegetarian.

MIKE

Coffee's made from vegetables.

SHELLY
I don't drink coffee, thanks. I'll just wait for Norman.

COOTIE
Where's Norman?

SHELLY
Well, he was arrested for carrying a concealed weapon, but he said it's OK because he has a permit. He's really a total-action freak, and he's very committed to the whole peace thing.

COOTIE
Oh.

MIKE
Well now . . .

COOTIE
How about that.

[*Fade out*]

End of scene 3

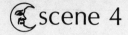scene 4

[NORMAN *is trying to read.* SHELLY *is under the table blowing bubbles.* MIKE *and* COOTIE *are playing chess.*]

MIKE

I still think you've said something, Norman. I mean it's got nothing to do with putting you on. If Dick said we didn't have a cat, all right, I mean he's got a right to think that but, I mean, it's really irresponsible of him to go running all over the place saying we don't.

NORMAN

Well, you turned off the lights that time when you came in. I was trying to read.

MIKE

Yeah, but that was the nitty-gritty, no-nonsense, down-to-earth needs of the moment because a cat just won't give birth with the lights on.

NORMAN

Dick says you don't have a cat.

MIKE

Will you listen to what I'm trying to tell you?

COOTIE

You can't move there.

MIKE

Why not?

COOTIE

Mate in thirty-four.

MIKE

Shit, I didn't see that. OK, your game.

[MIKE *and* COOTIE *start rearranging the pieces.*]

COOTIE

Yeah, you see, Dick gets these things and he'll tell you, like, we don't have a cat or something like that. We would've explained if you'd just come out and asked instead of getting all hostile and paranoid and thinking we were putting you on.

SHELLY

Wow, bubbles are really something else. I think they're maybe divine.

MIKE

Bubbles are divine, Shelly.

COOTIE
So's Bogart.

SHELLY
Oh, Bogart, wow.

COOTIE
You're pretty happy, aren't you, Shelly?

SHELLY
Oh . . . yeah. Like, it's the right foods. And being under the table.

MIKE
You gotta watch the paranoid thing, Norman.

NORMAN
You were putting me on about the cat.

MIKE
See, you got this very paranoid thing about the cat.

NORMAN
I have not . . .

COOTIE
And the worst thing is how you get all defensive about it every time we bring it up. We're not denying your

validity to doubt, Norman. We're not rejecting you as a human being. It's just you have a very paranoid personality because your father's a cop and that means you grew up in a very paranoid atmosphere.

SHELLY
Wow, your father's a cop?

NORMAN
Well, you know . . .

SHELLY
You never told me that. I think that's really great. My brother always wanted to be a cop.

COOTIE
My uncle's a cop.

MIKE
Yeah, that's right, our uncle's a cop.

NORMAN
That's what I mean, you see . . .

MIKE
What do you mean?

NORMAN
Well, I mean, you've got to go making fun of my father being a cop.

101

MIKE

Look, Norman, it just so happens our uncle is a cop and why the hell should you be the only one around here with a cop in the family. You see, you got paranoid again, thinking we're putting you on. I mean, we could do the same thing. How do we know your father's a cop? We don't. We trust you.

COOTIE

Yeah, and if you'd've been outer-directed maybe you'd've seen you got a lot in common with us. A lot more than you ever expected.

MIKE

Then maybe we could've prevented that whole tragic episode with the gun.

NORMAN

Yeah, well, I don't know about you guys.

MIKE

You're not trying to say it wasn't a tragic episode.

COOTIE

It was an abortion of academic freedom, pure and simple.

MIKE

Here! here!

COOTIE

I mean, when they can kick mathematics graduate
students out of school just for trying to murder a few
cops. . . . And, by the way, Norman, I've heard that
your being kicked out of school was the doing of the
Dean of Admissions, a man who is known far and wide
to be cornholing his widowed sister in the eye-sockets
regularly. . . .

MIKE

And without love.

COOTIE

And when the moon comes up he ties her to this
plank . . .

MIKE

Mel . . .

COOTIE

So put that in yer pipe and smoke it. And don't try to
tell us you enjoy having to schlepp down to the Hays
Bick every night to wash dishes for a dollar ten an hour.

NORMAN

Oh, I don't know.

SHELLY

Hey, are you guys brothers?

MIKE

Now there. Look at that, Norman. Shelly's wondering about the relationship between Mel and me, and instead of being all paranoid about it and going crazy wondering she comes right out and asks.

SHELLY

Hey, are you?

COOTIE

Yeah, we're brothers.

SHELLY

Wow, I didn't know that either. I keep learning all these things about you guys.

MIKE

See, everything's cool now. Everybody trusts each other. That's what it's all about.

NORMAN

Well, I mean, with washing dishes I get more time to read. I've been thinking a lot and I guess it's like Dick said. I was pretty irrelevant before. Mathematics is pretty irrelevant no matter how you look at it, and bad mathematics is about as irrelevant as you can get.

SHELLY

I left school after the first month. I'm not saying I'm

really relevant, yet, but like, some of my friends in school are really into bad scenes. School is evil. You can't find out where it's at when you're studying all the time to fit your head into exams. I'm getting to where I can read recipes all day and really get something out of it.

NORMAN

Yeah. I'm learning all this stuff about Vietnam. It's really something. I mean, I'm getting to the point where maybe I can do something really relevant about it.

MIKE

I wouldn't call that gun business relevant.

NORMAN

I was still in school when I thought of that.

SHELLY

Norman's got this fantastic idea.

NORMAN

Well, I haven't thought it all out yet . . .

SHELLY

No, Norman-baby, don't like close all up. It's the most relevant thing I ever heard of.

105

COOTIE

Jesus, Norman, how long have you been walking around with this idea all locked up inside you?

NORMAN

I didn't get it all at once. It sort of came in stages, but I think it's about right.

COOTIE

Man, you're gonna go crazy if you keep everything inside like that.

SHELLY

Tell them the idea, Norman.

NORMAN

Well, you see . . . [*Pause*] I'm gonna set myself on fire as a protest against the war.

[COOTIE *and* MIKE *look at him and exchange brief glances.*]

I've thought about it a lot. I mean, I've read I guess about a hundred books about the war and the more you read the more you see it's no one thing you can put your finger on. It's right in the middle of the whole system, like Dick said. I shouldn't've tried to kill those policemen, but I didn't know then they were part of the system like everything else. No one's got the right to take anyone else's life, that's what I've decided. But I've still got the right to take my own life for something I believe in.

SHELLY

I'm gonna burn with Norman. We're gonna burn together. We've thought it all through and, like, if he burns himself alone that's just one person. Everyone'll say he's insane, but if two of us do it . . . wow. Two people. What are they gonna say if two of us do it?

MIKE

[*Pause*] Three of us.

COOTIE

Four of us.

MIKE

You, too, huh?

COOTIE

It's the only way.

NORMAN

Hey, wait a minute. I've read a lot about the whole subject and I really know just why I'm gonna do it. I'm not just doing it for fun or anything. You can't just jump into it.

MIKE

Listen, Norman, you don't have to believe this if you don't want to, but it's the truth, on my honor. Me and Cootie talked about the same thing a year ago. We were all ready to burn ourselves . . .

COOTIE

It was more than a year ago.

MIKE

More than a year?

COOTIE

Almost a year and a half.

MIKE

That's right, a year and a half. Boy, time really goes quick.

COOTIE

It sure does.

MIKE

The thing is, we decided against it because we figured two isn't enough.

COOTIE

You know how the papers can lie. "Brothers Burn."

MIKE

Yeah, "Hippie Brothers in Suicide Pact." That kind of shit.

COOTIE

Think of it, though. With four of us.

NORMAN

You really want to do it?

MIKE

It's the only way.

NORMAN

I mean, I wasn't sure yet. I hadn't made up my mind definitely. I was still looking for another way.

SHELLY

No, Norman-baby, it's the only relevant gesture. Like you said.

[*Long pause.*]

NORMAN

OK.

MIKE

After the Christmas vacation.

109

COOTIE

No, no, after graduation. We'll study like mad and get fantastic grades and graduate with honors so they can't say we were cracking up or anything.

MIKE

Yeah, we'll get Phi Beta Kappa. I'd like to see them say we're insane when two Phi Beta Kappas go up in flames with the son of a policeman and the daughter of a . . . Hey, what does your father do?

SHELLY

Well, it's kind of funny. I mean, he's a pretty weird head in his way. He's got, like, six or seven jobs at any one time.

MIKE

That's okay Daughter of a weird head with six or seven jobs at any given time. That covers the whole spectrum.

NORMAN

What does your father do? I mean, I know your uncle's a policeman because I trust you, but you never said what your father did. I was curious. Like, if they bring our fathers into it what'll they say about you?

COOTIE

He's a trapper.

SHELLY

Wow, that's really something else. Like, a fur trapper?

COOTIE

Furs and hides, you know. Rabbit and mink and muskrat and beaver and elk and reindeer and seal. Some otter. Penguin.

SHELLY

Wow, penguin.

COOTIE

Well, you know, he works the Great Northwest Territory up to the mouth of the St. Lawrence seaway, and over to the Aleutians.

SHELLY

Boy, this'll really blow everyone's mind.

MIKE

Yeah, this'll make everyone think twice, all right.

COOTIE

You know, we can't tell anyone about this. If word gets out they'll send squads of police around here and we'll get arrested and put under psychiatric observation and we'll get subjected to a battery of tests that make you look nuts no matter how you answer.

NORMAN
I won't say anything.

SHELLY
Oh, wow, like you don't even have to worry about me.

NORMAN
I didn't even know there were any trappers left.

[*A knock on the door.*]

MIKE
Come in.

VOICE
C'mon, c'mon, open up in there.

[MIKE *opens the door and finds two cops standing there.* BREAM *is elderly and* EFFING *is young.*]

BREAM
You live here?

MIKE
Yes, sir.

BREAM
Look, you know what I mean, you and who else.

MIKE

Well, there's me and my brother Cootie . . . um, Mel, and there's Norman, Dick, Bob, Kathy, and Ruth.

BREAM

Kathy and Ruth, huh? Those are girl's names.

MIKE

Kathy and Ruth are both girls, sir.

BREAM

Don't block the doorway.

[MIKE *stands aside as* BREAM *and* EFFING *enter.* EFFING *wanders around the room, inspecting.*]

[*Indicating Shelly*] Which one's she? You Kathy or Ruth?

SHELLY

I'm Shelly.

BREAM

Shelly, huh? You didn't say nothin' about no Shelly.

MIKE

She doesn't live here, sir.

BREAM
Visiting?

SHELLY
I'm with Norman.

BREAM
You're Norman, huh?

NORMAN
She's my girl friend.

BREAM
Good, we got that straight.

EFFING
Hey, Bream, this here's a map of Europe.

BREAM
Yeah. Now listen. There's been a complaint from the people across there. I know you kids are students and you probably think you own the goddamn country, but I got some news for you. There's laws around here and you gotta obey them just like everyone else.

MIKE
We appreciate that, sir.

EFFING
Hey, Bream, look at all them milk bottles.

BREAM

Yeah. Now listen. I don't want to hear any more complaints about you guys. I'm a reasonable man, which is something you can get verified by askin' anyone on the force, but when I gotta put up with a lotta stupid complaints I can cause trouble, and I mean real trouble, with a capital T.

EFFING

Hey, look at all them dishes in the sink, Bream.

BREAM

Yeah.

NORMAN

What was the complaint?

BREAM

What do you mean, what was the complaint? The complaint was guys and girls parading around in here bare-ass. Now look, I'm not the kind of dumb cop that goes around throwing his weight everywhere to prove he's some kind of big shot. I don't need to, you follow me. I know what I know and I know what I don't know, and one of the things I know I don't know is what the hell the kids are up to nowadays, but OK. That's my problem. If you wanna run around naked that's OK by me, and I hope you kids take note of the fact that I'm winking one eye when it comes to the law about cohabitation.

MIKE

We appreciate that fact, sir. It was the first thing we noticed.

COOTIE

I sure appreciate it. I think I can speak for Norman and Shelly, and if any of the other guys were here they'd appreciate it a lot.

MIKE

I mean it's not as if we underestimate the life of a cop. For chrissakes, I mean, our uncle's a cop. His father's a cop. A lot of us around here are pretty close to the world of cops.

BREAM

You got cops in the family?

EFFING

Hey, Bream, look at this heater.

BREAM

Yeah.

MIKE

It's not like we don't know what you guys have to put up with. It can be a pretty crappy job.

BREAM

I don't know . . .

MIKE

I'm not saying it doesn't have its rewards. My uncle's
life is full of rewards. His father's life is very
meaningful.

BREAM

Yeah, that's what I mean.

[COOTIE *gets up and starts to leave the room.*]

EFFING

Hey, Bream, the kid's leaving the room.

COOTIE

I got a call from nature.

BREAM

That's legit. You go ahead, kid.

[COOTIE *goes out the front door.*]

EFFING

Hey, Bream, the kid says he's going to the euphemism
and what if he's got some stuff on him or something. He
can flush it down and come back clean.

117

BREAM

He's okay.

EFFING

Jesus, Bream. Sir.

BREAM

The guy's new on the job. He don't know the score yet.

MIKE

You know how some people exaggerate. I mean, look what they say in the papers about you guys. Maybe, like after a shower we'll come in here to get an anchovy snack or chocolate milk or something, and we forget to put something on . . .

EFFING

Look at that, Bream, the girl keeps sitting under there . . .

BREAM

Goddamnit, Effing, who's in charge around here?

EFFING

But she's sitting under there . . .

BREAM

Did we come here to investigate a complaint about a girl sitting under the table?

118

EFFING
No, sir, but . . .

BREAM
The girl happens to be well within her rights as a
taxpaying citizen of the community to sit under any
table she wants, and until we get complaints about her
sitting under there we leave her alone. Understand?

EFFING
Yeah, yeah, yeah . . .

SHELLY
Thanks.

BREAM
That's okay, lady. The kid's a rookie. They give us pros
a bad name. Now let me tell you something about the
people complaining about you. They look in here and
see you guys bare-assed and they're complaining because
they're so sick of looking at each other they gotta go
spying on you. We know about them people. They're
strict Roman Catholics. Twelve kids in four rooms. The
old man can't keep it in his pants for ten minutes
running. So they got troubles, right, and everyone that's
got troubles wants to give troubles to someone else. So
they make a complaint, and that's well within their
rights as law-abiding citizens of this community. I got
enough troubles without their goddamn complaints. I

119

got enough to do watching the Vietnam freaks and the
niggers and the loonies going up on buildings with
high-power rifles picking off everyone down below. Let
me give you some good advice. Get curtains. They got
some fiber glass curtains at Woolworth's, you can't tell
them from real cotton. Twelve dollars and fifty cents a
pair and they come in eight colors, plain and patterned.
You get some curtain rods for a dollar sixty-nine apiece
and for a total of twenty-eight dollars and thirty-eight
cents you save yourself from a lot of crazy neighbors. If
you can't afford twenty-eight dollars and thirty-eight
cents, get some gingham, thirty-nine cents a yard at
Penny's. Measure your windows and allow a foot extra
at each end. All you gotta do is take up a three-inch
hem at each end, fold it over once, and hand stitch. A
couple of curtain rings and you're in business. Can you
remember that, or d'you want me to write it down?

SHELLY
Hey, yeah, would you do that?

[BREAM *takes out a notebook and starts to write.*
EFFING *is nervous.*]

EFFING
The kid's been gone a long time.

BREAM
I got eyes, Effing.

EFFING

Yeah, yeah, yeah, OK.

BREAM

(Writing) So, what are you kids gonna do with yourselves? *(Pause)* Am I being nosy or something?

MIKE

No, I mean, there's a lot of opportunities all over the place. We're not jumping into anything without we've looked the whole thing over.

BREAM

Smart kids. Boy, that's really something. Cop sending his kid to college. They must pay him pretty good, huh?

NORMAN

I guess so.

BREAM

Yeah, what's he, a sergeant . . . lieutenant or something?

NORMAN

He's Chief of Police for Buffalo County.

BREAM

[*Whistles*] Whew! Pretty good. That shut me up OK. Chief of Police. Oh boy, that's really something.

121

NORMAN
It's just his job, you know.

BREAM
Look, ah, here's your instructions. I want them up by Wednesday. Any complaints after that and all of you guys'll be in court, father or no father, you understand me? This ain't Buffalo.

MIKE
Yes, sir.

NORMAN
OK.

[COOTIE *returns and stands in the door. There's a pause.*]

COOTIE
That's better.

End of scene 4 and Act One

ACT TWO

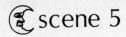scene 5

[RUTH *is scraping some cat food into a bowl. A cat comes in and eats.* RUTH *keeps glancing at her watch.*]

RUTH
Kitty-kitty-kitty-kitty-kitty. Chomp, chomp. Good girl. Make a lot of milk for the kitties.

[KATHY *comes in from the hall and throws herself down on a chair.*]

KATHY
Oh, Jesus, Ruth, how am I ever gonna tell him?

RUTH
Who?

KATHY
Bob, for chrissakes. Who else?

RUTH
Well, how should I know?

KATHY

I never slept with Dick. I know you got the idea I did, but it's not true. He never got all the way.

RUTH

OK.

KATHY

Yet. I'm not saying I wouldn't like to.

RUTH

So go ahead.

KATHY

Well don't try to pretend it doesn't mean anything to you. You know as well as I do it'll kill Bob if he ever finds out I'm even thinking of sleeping with Dick.

RUTH

That's how it goes.

KATHY

Ruthie, look, we've known each other since freshman year. I can tell when you're thinking something. This is really a big decision I've gotta make. What am I gonna do about Bob? I mean, it feels like maybe we're, you know, finished, but I like the guy. I really like him a lot and I respect his music. But I know he could never relate to me as a friend. It's gotta be tied up with sex. I mean, Richard really seems to dig me, but I don't know. He's pretty together. He's not the kind of guy you could really do something big for. Not like Bob.

RUTH

Oh, for shit's sake, Kathy, Dick is a fucking parasite.

KATHY

That's not fair, Ruth.

RUTH

Fair, shit. Do you know what that guy's doing to get into graduate school? You ever heard of Professor Roper in the Eastern studies department?

KATHY

He's Dick's tutor.

RUTH

Yeah, and he also happens to be queer as a three-dollar bill, and Dick is fucking his wife to keep her quiet so good old Roper can suck cock with all those graduate students from Thailand or Malaya, or whatever the hell they are.

KATHY

Who said?

127

RUTH

Who said? For chrissakes, Kathy, the whole goddamn school knows about it. Dirty Dicky.

KATHY

That's why?

RUTH

Yeah, what else? I mean, the guy washes eight times a day.

KATHY

Oh, man, how long have you guys known about this? I mean, like why didn't anyone ever tell me? You can't just let him screw up his future like that. Hasn't anyone tried to do anything about it?

RUTH

Like tell him Mrs. Roper's got clap?

KATHY

Ruthie, the guy must be really suffering.

RUTH

Oh shit, Kathy, let's not have the big savior thing.

KATHY

That's not very funny.

RUTH

Look, we're all gonna graduate pretty soon, and we're all gonna go away, and probably we'll never see each other again except maybe like at Christmas or something. So why don't you worry about yourself and never mind about Dick and Bob. They'll be OK.

KATHY

Boy, you sure have changed, Ruth. I don't know. You sure have changed.

[BOB *comes through front door carrying books.*]

BOB

I don't believe it. It's incredible. You know what happened today in counterpoint class? Remember I was telling you about Eric Shatz?

RUTH

. . . three armpits. . . ?

BOB

The very one.

KATHY

[*Nicely*] Bob . . .

[BOB, *who has gone to the icebox to steal some of*
DICK's *hamburgers, stops short in whatever gesture he*

is holding, only for a moment though, just long enough to cut KATHY. *When he resumes his story, he is talking only to* RUTH, *who is wrapping a Christmas present.*]

BOB

Today Shatz turned in this perfect, spotless, clean counterpoint exercise. I mean, for someone as filthy as Shatz, that's a miracle. They say his high-school yearbook voted him "The Most Likely to Attract Infectious Disease."

[BOB *has the hamburgers out by now.* KATHY, *being all nice, takes the hamburgers from him, indicating that she'll cook.* BOB *goes away from her and sits with* RUTH.]

He picks his nose and squeezes his pimples right there in class, and his counterpoint exercises have to be seen to be believed. He writes them in pencil, and if he makes a mistake or something, he spits on his eraser and rubs the paper about a hundred times . . . per note, so by the time he hands it to Professor Bolin, it's just this gray sludge with lots of little black things swimming around on it. Anyway, about a week ago, when Shatz handed over his work, Professor Bolin put on a pair of gloves before he'd take it, so Shatz must've got the message and this week when Bolin called for homework, Shatz set this beautiful, clean exercise down on the piano. We couldn't believe it. Bolin just sat there staring at it, and we all sat staring at Bolin, and after about ten minutes, no shit, it took that long, Bolin turned to us and said, "Free will is an illusion." Isn't that too much?

KATHY

Bob, can I talk to you. . . ?

[BOB *ignores her.*]

BOB

The thing is, Bolin's got a Ph.D. He's also written two books and a couple of hundred symphonies and string quartets and they say he taught himself twenty-two languages in four hours or something . . .

KATHY

Please, Bob, I want to talk to you . . .

BOB

And another thing, Bolin's wife got drunk at a faculty party for the music department last year and she yelled, "Fuck Shönberg, I get it off with Miles Davis," and then she went and laid the only black professor in the school, which all goes to show that when Bolin tells you free will is an illusion . . . you better believe it.

KATHY

[*Pointed*] Bob, I would like to talk to you . . .

131

BOB

Hey, Ruth, did I ever tell you the one about the guy
that died and came back to life as Job?

KATHY

Oh don't start that shit again.

BOB

Again? It started over a month ago. I mean, even Bolin
caught on after two lessons. Of course he still makes me
walk around the music building every time I put down
parallel fifths, but that's how it goes, life is trying at the
best of times, every cloud has a silver lining, a stitch in
time saves nine . . .

[RUTH *looks at her watch.*]

RUTH

I've gotta go.

BOB

Did I say something?

RUTH

No. Kathy wants to talk to you about sleeping with
Dick.

KATHY

Ruth . . . bitch!

[RUTH *goes out the front door, grabbing her coat on the way.*]

BOB

[*Pause*] Meanwhile, back at the ranch . . . You'll never believe this, but when I came in just now, I didn't expect that. Bedbugs, maybe. Thermonuclear war . . .

KATHY

She had no right.

BOB

I'm trying to think of something appropriate to say, like "Name the first one after me." That's Job. J-O-B. Job.

KATHY

Please, Bob, can I say something . . .

BOB

Do you have trouble pronouncing the name Job?

KATHY

Jesus Christ, you're impossible.

BOB

Ah, yes, but I exist, nonetheless.

KATHY

You've just cut me right out. You're not even trying to relate to me any more. [*Pause*] Well, you're not.

BOB

No, Kathy. The fact is, I like you a lot. I, um, sort of love you, if you know what I mean.

KATHY

I don't really want to sleep with Dick.

BOB

Then don't.

KATHY

It's just, he tried to get me that night after the demonstration.

BOB

I know. He told me.

KATHY

That shit.

BOB

I thought it was pretty good of him.

KATHY

He never got into me, you know.

BOB

That's nice.

KATHY

Oh, Bob, I'm sorry.

BOB

If Bob were around I'm sure he'd forgive you.

KATHY

What'll we do?

BOB

What do you mean? Like study or something?

KATHY

Bob, how does it stand? Is it . . . it's over, isn't it?

BOB

Between us, you mean?

KATHY

Yes.

BOB

If that's what you want.

KATHY

Of course I don't want it. I love you a lot.

BOB

OK, so let's study for Phil 720.

KATHY

Oh, for chrissakes, show some emotion. I don't know where I'm at with you half the time.

BOB

Look, what's the big hang-up? If you want to stay with me, OK. If you want to move into Dick's room, go ahead. If you don't know for sure stay one night with me and one night with him till you start feeling a definite preference for one of us . . .

KATHY

Jesus Christ, Bob, what's the matter with you?

BOB

I'm Job. Bob's dead.

[KATHY *flounces down the hall, slamming the door behind her. She reenters almost immediately to say . . .*]

KATHY

If you want me, I'll be in Dick's room.

BOB

OK.

[KATHY *is gone.* BOB *goes to the stack of floor tiles, picks up a few. He looks at the unfinished floor.* BOB *stares ahead. Another knock.* BOB *speaks in a sort of trance.*]

Come in.

[*Another knock.* BOB *comes out of it.*]

The door's open. Come in.

[*The door opens slowly. Standing there is a middle-aged man. He's swaying a little and carries a bottle of rye. He is Bob's uncle,* MURRY.]

MURRY
Can I come in?

BOB
[*Surprised, friendly*] Murry, what the hell are you doing here?

MURRY
A guy travels a couple a hundred miles to see his nephew, maybe he can come in, huh?

BOB
Yeah, yeah, come in. Come on, sit down.

MURRY
I bet you're surprised to see me. Maybe a little happy?

137

BOB

Well, yeah, I mean, I haven't seen you for a couple of thousand years or something.

MURRY

It's longer than that since you wrote. Hey, Bobby-boy, Bobby-boy.

[MURRY *ruffles* BOB*'s hair. This annoys* BOB.]

You got long hair.

BOB

It keeps growing.

MURRY

Just like your mother, huh! Proud.

BOB

[*Distant*] How long you in town for?

MURRY

Oh, you know, business. Hey, you want a drink?

BOB

No thanks. You go ahead.

[*He gets* MURRY *a glass.* MURRY *is looking around.*]

MURRY

You drink a lotta milk, huh?

BOB

Yeah.

[*They look at each other and laugh.*]

MURRY

Where did you find that goddamned icebox?

BOB

You like it?

MURRY

Oh Jesus, Bobby, Bobby-boy, is this how you been living?

BOB

[*Long pause*] Yeah.

MURRY

Why didn't you tell me. Write a letter, that's all. Say, "Murry, I need a little cash." I would've sent you some money for a decent refrigerator.

BOB

Murry, I'm living OK.

MURRY

Just like your mother. She was always proud.

[MURRY *drinks.* BOB *stiffens imperceptibly at the use of the past tense.*]

Yeah, I came through New York.

BOB

[*Guarded*] How's the kids?

MURRY

Huh? Oh, yeah. They're fine. Keep asking about you.

BOB

Auntie Stella?

MURRY

Oh, you know, she's fine. We got a new house.

BOB

Great.

MURRY

Yeah. You gotta come and visit us, huh? Don't worry about money. I give you the tickets, you fly out and stay with us. The kids'd love to see you.

BOB

Yeah, yeah, great. You know, maybe this summer, you know, after I graduate.

MURRY

I saw your mother in New York.

BOB

She OK?

MURRY

Yeah, yeah, sure. She'd maybe like a letter every now and then. Your own mother.

BOB

It's not like that, Murry. When I see her I see her.

MURRY

[*Shivers*] Jesus Christ. [*He drinks*]

BOB

You OK?

MURRY

Sit down, Bobby-boy.

BOB

I'm OK like this.

MURRY

I got something to tell you, you should maybe be sitting down when I tell you.

[BOB *sits.* MURRY *pulls his chair close and takes* BOB*'s head in his hands.* BOB *is stiff.*]

Bobby-boy, oh Bobby. I'd like to see more of you, kid. Me and the family. You maybe come out and visit, huh?

BOB

[*Flat*] What's happened, Murry?

MURRY

How am I supposed to tell you?

[*The phone rings.*]

BOB

Hang on a second. [HE *answers phone*] Hello? [*Pause*] No, he's not here. [*Pause*] No, he won't be back 'cause he's dead. [*Pause*] Don't worry, he didn't suffer, not much, anyway. [*Pause*] No of course we don't want the phone disconnected, we're still living here. Hey, who is this, anyway? [*Pause*] Oh. [*To* MURRY] Telephone Company.

MURRY

Tell them to call back later.

BOB

[*Into phone*] Yeah, listen, I'll call you back a . . .
[*Pause, to* MURRY] They're getting the supervisor.

MURRY

God help me, of all times they should call you now.

BOB

[*Into phone*] Yeah, hello . . . yeah . . . yeah . . . no, I
mean, no, I explained all this to the operator. [*Pause*]
Oh, well, I didn't know it wasn't the operator. [*Pause*]
Yeah, but look, how am I supposed to have known that
it was a controller trainee just from the voice? You can't
tell me controller trainees have special voices. [*Pause*]
I'm not angry. [*Pause*] OK, go ahead. [*Pause*] Yes, I
know that. [*Pause*] I said, "I know that." I know that
you are the supervisor because the operator . . . no, wait
a minute, what did you say she was . . . [*Pause*] the
controller trainee, that's the one . . . [*Pause*] Look,
willya be quiet for a minute and let me explain . . .
[*Pause*] I'm not angry. [*Pause*] I'm not being rude.
[*Pause*] I am not. I'm just trying to explain that when I
spoke to the controller trainee, she ended by saying that
the supervisor wanted to speak to me, and then you
came on the phone, and that's how I know you're the
supervisor, so when you said, "This is the supervisor
speaking," you didn't have to because I already knew . . .
never mind, forget it. What do you want?

143

MURRY

For God's sake, tell her to call back later, Bobby. I gotta tell you something.

BOB

[*Into phone*] Huh? No, I'm trying to listen to two things at once . . . I got my uncle here. [*Pause, polite*] No, I would say we make an average number of calls, but that's just a guess, because I don't know how many calls most people make. [*Pause*] Yeah, but it's not like any of us makes a lot of calls, it's just, I don't know, there's a lot of people living here and each of us makes an average number of calls so it adds up to a lot.

MURRY

Not now, Jesus Christ, Bobby, not now . . .

BOB

Look, Miss Supervisor . . . [*Pause*] Oh, sorry . . . *Mrs. Tomalson,* I got my uncle here and he's trying to tell me . . .

[BOB *suddenly realizes what he's saying, lowers the receiver, and looks at* MURRY. *Then, to escape the moment, he takes the receiver back to his ear and, watching* MURRY *all the while, speaks to the voice at the other end.*]

Hey, how do you guys know how many calls we're making? You got a special department down there to spy on us just so you can try to sell us another phone? Mrs. Tomalson, I'm a taxpayer and I want to tell you that you have a fucking nerve . . .

[MURRY *approaches* BOB.]

[*To* MURRY] You wouldn't believe this woman, she's really twisted.

[MURRY *takes the receiver from* BOB *and sets it back in its cradle. They stare at each other.* MURRY *reaches up to touch* BOB*'s face.* BOB *turns away.*]

MURRY
. . . Bobby . . .

BOB
[*Long pause*] Cancer.

[MURRY *nods.* BOB *doesn't see him.*]

How long's she got?

MURRY
A week, Two weeks. I don't know. Any time now.

BOB
Those operations . . . kidney trouble. Oh, shit, why didn't someone tell me?

MURRY

You got your studies, we should worry you to death?

BOB

[*Flat*] Fuck you all.

MURRY

I thought . . . I thought maybe you and me fly to New York tonight.

BOB

Yeah, get in there quick for the payoff. That'll be just great.

MURRY

She don't know yet.

BOB

Yeah. "Hi, Mom, I just came flying in with Murry a couple of weeks before Christmas vacation to see you for no good reason." You think she won't guess?

MURRY

She doesn't have to. We can always tell her something.

BOB

You planning to keep it from her, too? I bet it's the first thing she thought of. Two years. She had that first

146

operation two years ago. She's been dying for two years and I didn't even fucking know it.

MURRY

That's it, Bobby. [*Pause*] Life is full of shit.

BOB

[*Pause*] I'll pack some stuff. No, you stay here. I want to be alone.

[BOB *goes down the hall.* MURRY *sits. Very short pause, then* MIKE *and* COOTIE *burst in through the front door, laden with Christmas presents. They see* MURRY, *cross the kitchen to the hall door, exit, and start arguing loudly just outside in the hallway. After a moment they reenter,* MIKE *leading. Deferential.*]

MIKE

Me and my friend were wondering if you could settle a little argument for us.

MURRY

What?

MIKE

Were you or weren't you the guy behind the bar in Key Largo, starring Humphrey Bogart and Edward G. Robinson?

MURRY

I'm Bob's uncle.

MIKE

[*To* COOTIE] He's Bob's uncle.

COOTIE

Are you a for-real uncle?

MURRY

[*Confused*] Yeah, yeah, I'm his uncle.

COOTIE

Maternal or paternal.

MURRY

I'm related to Bob through his mother. She was . . .
she's my sister.

MIKE

That means you and him have different names.

MURRY

Yeah, he's a Rettie, I'm a Golden.

MIKE

That's a pretty convincing story, mister.

COOTIE
Most of the pieces fit pretty good.

[MIKE *and* COOTIE *start toward the hall.* SHELLY *comes in the front door.*]

SHELLY
Hi, everyone.

MIKE
Hiya, Shelly.

COOTIE
Good old Shelly, hiya.

[MIKE *and* COOTIE *are gone down the hall.*]

SHELLY
Hey . . . Excuse me, do you know if Norman's here?

MURRY
I don't know who Norman is.

SHELLY
One of the guys here. I mean, like he lives here. You someone's father?

MURRY
I'm Bob's uncle.

SHELLY

Bob? Oh, yeah, Job.

[SHELLY *sits under the table.*]

I'm waiting for Norman. Hey, are you, like, a for-real uncle?

MURRY

You kids keep asking that.

SHELLY

You don't think of him with an uncle.

MURRY

Look, if you don't want me to stay in here, I'll go and help Bob.

SHELLY

No, you stay here. Like, I enjoy company. Hey, is he here?

MURRY

I'm afraid I don't know your friend Norman.

SHELLY

I mean Job. Your nephew.

MURRY

Yes, he's here. I'm waiting for him.

SHELLY

He's, like, in here somewhere? Inside the apartment?

MURRY

Yes. Look, you want to go down and ask him about Norman, go ahead.

SHELLY

Is he in the toilet?

MURRY

He's in his room.

SHELLY

Wow, that's, like, really weird.

MURRY

He's just packing, that's all.

SHELLY

Yeah, but I mean, if you're his for-real uncle how come you're like sitting in here when he's down there?

MURRY

Look, he . . . [*Weeping softly*] . . . I don't know.

SHELLY

Hey, you're really crying like crazy. What's the matter? I thought you were, like, waiting for him to come back here, you know, like, to the apartment or something. I just wanted to know because I'm waiting for Norman to come back so I thought we could maybe sit here together waiting and that would be something we had in common, then you told me he was in his room packing and everything and I thought that was sorta weird 'cause if you're like his for-real uncle you could just go down there and be with him. Why's he packing?

BOB
[*Entering with bag*] Okay. I'm ready.

SHELLY
Hey, Job, you going away?

BOB
I'll be back in a few days.

SHELLY
Like, you mean, you're not just going home early for Christmas vacation.

BOB
No.

SHELLY
Oh. OK. Hey, Merry Christmas, you guys.

BOB
Merry Christmas.

152

MURRY

Merry Christmas.

[DICK *comes in through the front door.* BOB *and* MURRY *start out.* DICK *is baffled.*]

DICK

Hey, you going?

BOB

Yeah. Kathy's in your room. [*Pause*] She doesn't like it from behind.

[BOB *and* MURRY *are gone.*]

DICK

Where's he going?

SHELLY

I don't know, but the guy with him is his for-real uncle and he's a weird head.

[KATHY *comes into the kitchen.*]

KATHY

Hey, did Bob just go out?

SHELLY

Wow, he didn't even tell you?

153

DICK

He left with his uncle.

KATHY

Uncle?

SHELLY

Yeah, like it's his for-real uncle, I'm pretty sure.

KATHY

Jesus, why didn't he say something. I mean, I been waiting for him down there . . .

SHELLY

Well, the uncle said Job went down to his room to pack, and, I mean, like if you were in there with him and he started putting a lot of socks and underwear and toilet stuff in a suitcase you should've got suspicious and asked him something, like where's he going.

KATHY

Look, I went to the bathroom, OK?

SHELLY

Ya didn't flush.

KATHY

Mind your own fucking business, Shelly. What does he expect me to do? How can I make plans for the

154

Christmas vacation if he just . . . shit, he could've said something.

[DICK, *in a feeble attempt to avoid* KATHY*'s rage, tries to sneak out down the hallway.*]

And listen, you, you have a lot of nerve telling him about that night.

DICK
I didn't say anything.

KATHY
He said you told him.

DICK
Honest, Kathy, I never did.

KATHY
[*Vague*] I'm really getting to hate this place.

[KATHY *starts down the hall.* DICK *starts after her.*]

DICK
Kathy!

[*Before* DICK *can get down the hall,* RUTH *rushes in through the front door, breathless.*]

RUTH

Oh, wow, have I ever had the most fantastic experience!

[DICK *goes down the hall, slamming the door.*]

[*Yelling*] You're a shit, Dick.

SHELLY

You seen Norman?

RUTH

Oh, hi, Shelly. Hey, let me tell you about what just happened to me. It really blew my mind.

[*From down the hall, we hear voices singing.*]

MIKE & COOTIE

[*Singing, offstage*]
WE WISH YOU A MERRY CHRISTMAS
WE WISH YOU A MERRY CHRISTMAS
WE WISH YOU A MERRY CHRISTMAS
WE WISH YOU A MERRY CHRISTMAS
WE WISH YOU A MERRY CHRISTMAS
WE WISH YOU A MERRY CHRISTMAS
WE WISH YOU A MERRY CHRISTMAS
WE WISH YOU A MERRY CHRISTMAS . . .
AND . . .

156

[MIKE *and* COOTIE *rush in from the hall dressed in Santa Claus costumes and end the song.*]

. . . A HAPPY NEW YEAR.

MIKE

We got a present for you, Ruth.

SHELLY

Hey, where'd you get those?

COOTIE

We're doing collections this year. Yep.

MIKE

You want to see the great old present we got ya?

RUTH

I was just gonna tell Shelly what happened when I went to see Quinn. You know Quinn, the albino dwarf . . .

MIKE

Oh, yeah, old Quinn.

COOTIE

Good old Quinn.

RUTH

Yeah, right. Well I had to see him about homework for

the Christmas vacation and, I mean, like, he was the last person I wanted to see. I always thought he was a vicious little bastard. I mean, he can be pretty shitty.

MIKE
They say he shot a man in Abilene.

COOTIE
In the back.

RUTH
Listen, willya. I went into his office and he's standing by the window, you know, three-feet high and everything. I thought he was probably gonna ask why I wasn't doing any homework, and I had this whole speech worked out about how I thought he was a pretentious little snot and how I frankly didn't give a shit about philosophy and even less of a shit about him, if that's possible and . . . oh, you know, I was really going to kill him. Anyway, he told me to come over to the window, so I came over and we both stood there looking out. Snow everywhere, like, white wherever you looked and a lot of snow coming down like in those paperweights you shake up, and there's all these kids down below coming out of the building, all little lumps moving across the white in slow motion, and we're looking at them, just the two of us for, I don't know, about a minute or two, and then he just turns to me, like without any warning, and says this incredibly beautiful thing . . .

MIKE

Hey, don't you want to see the nifty present we got ya?

RUTH

Let me tell you what the guy said, willya?

MIKE

Right, you tell us what Quinn said, then we'll show you the present.

RUTH

Yeah.

MIKE

Will you look at the present first, then tell us what Quinn said?

RUTH

For Christ's sake, stop fucking around and listen.

MIKE

All right, what did Quinn say?

COOTIE

Good old Quinn.

[As RUTH *starts to speak,* KATHY *stomps into the room with a hastily packed suitcase, wearing an unbuttoned coat over whatever she was wearing just before. She doesn't look at the others. She just goes out the front door. A second later,* DICK *rushes into the kitchen, struggling into a jacket. He stops momentarily when he sees them all watching him. He says nothing. He goes out the front door after* KATHY. *The others all look at each other. After a longish pause,* MIKE *turns to* RUTH.]

MIKE
You were saying about Quinn?

[*Blackout.*]

End of scene 5

☾scene 6

[*Most of the posters are down. A bare feeling. Around graduation. There's some letters on the table.* RUTH, *alone, is reading her letter.* DICK *comes in from outside, dressed for warm weather, perhaps carrying a box. He opens the icebox.*]

DICK
Shit, nothing left.

RUTH
We cleaned it.

DICK
Anyone gone yet?

RUTH
No. Why don't you look at your grades?

DICK
[*Opens letter*] Jesus.

RUTH

Bad?

DICK

Fucking awful.

RUTH

Do you graduate?

DICK

Yeah, just.

RUTH

They sent Kathy's grades here.

DICK

That was tactful.

RUTH

Maybe she'll be around to pick them up. I got into graduate school.

DICK

Great.

RUTH

Philosophy.

DICK

Philosophy?

RUTH

Yeah! [*Pause*] I mean, you know, why not?

[DICK *starts toward the hall.*]

Hey, Dick, I don't get it. You know that day she left, just before Christmas . . . did you get into her?

DICK

How fucking low can you stoop, Ruth?

RUTH

No, I mean, you know, just, she must've done something to fuck you up this bad.

DICK

Kathy did not fuck me up.

RUTH

Yeah, well, ever since she left you've been looking like really terrible. You never even studied for finals. I mean, you were the academic head around here. Hey, you did get her, didn't you, and I bet she told you you were the first guy that ever turned her on.

163

[DICK *starts out again.*]

Did she? Oh, come off it, Dick, I just . . . I thought we were friends.

DICK

You know what that goddamn fucking little cunt told me? Just before she left? She told me I was screwing Roper's wife. Me, screwing Roper's wife.

RUTH

Well, you know Kathy.

DICK

She said everybody in the whole fucking school knew about it. It got back to Roper.

RUTH

Wow, I bet he was pretty pissed off, huh?

DICK

He was pretty good about it, considering. He pulled me in after a tutorial and gave me the old "Richard, my boy" speech. He thought I started the rumor. Me. Shit. "Richard, my boy, it's said you're doing unenviable things to my wife. My boy, that particular assignment has already been well seen to. It's not like you to claim credit for someone else's work." You ever tried to do a paper for someone who thinks you've been saying you're screwing his wife? Shit. Poor old fairy. Boy, what a fucking mess.

[BOB *comes in the front door.*]

RUTH
Hey, Bob, you got your grades.

BOB
Oh, yeah. [*He looks*]

RUTH
How'd you do?

BOB
OK. This for Kathy?

RUTH
Yeah.

[BOB *starts to open* KATHY*'s letter.*]

Hey, that's private property.

BOB
What the fuck's gotten into you all of a sudden. [*Reads*]
A, A, A, A . . . B minus. B minus in Poetry 210. Man,
she really went to pieces without us. I hope she hasn't
had a nervous breakdown or anything. Whew, B minus.

[*A knock on the door.* DICK *opens it. It's* LUCKY.]

LUCKY

Listen. I just seen Mr. Willis. He wants you out by tomorrow night.

BOB

How ya been, Lucky?

LUCKY

What? Oh, yeah. Well, if you want a hand, you know where to find me.

RUTH

Thanks a lot, buddy.

LUCKY

Don't get fresh, girlie. Don't give me lip. You can talk how you want when you're with your own, but you show a little respect when you're with Lucky. Smart alecks. Think you know everything, but you don't. You don't know anything about living downstairs. I know what it's like. I live downstairs. Thinking you know everything.

BOB

Yeah, lots of times.

DICK
Don't worry, we took care of it.

LUCKY
Huh?

DICK
We did like you said. Got rid of those plastic garbage cans and got some galvanized aluminum.

LUCKY
All right, that's what I mean. Now, if you want any help, I'll tell you what you do. You come downstairs. OK?

[*As* LUCKY *goes. We see him look around and call,* "*Kitty-Kitty.*"]

RUTH
Guess I'll pack.

[RUTH *gets up to leave.* DICK *starts taking down one of his posters.*]

BOB
Where's everyone?

RUTH
Mike and Mel went out with Norman. They're meeting

167

Shelly at the flicks. *Casablanca.* You should see the marks they got. They're both magna cum.

DICK
Magna cum. Sneaky bastards.

RUTH
Yep.

[RUTH *goes out down hall.*]

DICK
You staying for graduation?

BOB
No, you?

DICK
[*Shakes head no*] Hey, you really going into the army?

BOB
Yeah, as a hostage. I don't know. What are you doing?

DICK
Shit, I don't know.

BOB
Anything lined up for the summer?

DICK

Yeah, delivering milk. It's your friendly college
graduate, Mrs. Miller. "Such a shame, the boy went to
college." Maybe I'll get sterilized, save any kids having
to go through all this. She really was a bitch, you know.

BOB

I guess so.

DICK

Guess so, shit, I hope she gets cancer of the tits and
suffers like crazy while she's dying. Honest to Christ,
she's the first person I ever met I could really kill.

BOB

Yeah.

DICK

Oh, great humility scene.

BOB

No, it's just, you know, that's how it goes.

DICK

You know something, Bob? You know what's wrong
with you?

BOB

I been waiting all this time for someone to tell me. What's wrong with me, Dick?

DICK

You let her get your balls, Bob.

BOB

That was pretty careless, wasn't it?

DICK

No shit, Bob. I remember when you got stung by that bee in the humanities quadrangle. I always wondered about that. I mean, you're supposed to yell when something like that happens. You don't stand there wondering if you should say something. You're really dead, you know.

BOB

Yeah, well, that's what I was trying to tell everyone right before Christmas. I thought I might just try it out, you know, being dead. Didn't feel any different.

DICK

I don't get it.

BOB

No, it's a pretty weird thing.

DICK
I gotta pack.

BOB
Yeah.

[DICK *leaves the room.* MIKE *and* COOTIE *burst in through the front door, panting heavily.*]

MIKE
Oh shit, man, we've really had it. Christ, how could the guy do it? I thought he was kidding.

[RUTH *comes in with a small suitcase.*]

RUTH
Hey, you guys better hurry up and pack. We gotta be out of here tomorrow.

COOTIE
Ruth, sit down, huh. Something pretty bad just happened. Seriously, no shitting around.

RUTH
Where's Norman?

COOTIE
Norman's . . . he just . . . oh shit.

MIKE

He set himself on fire.

BOB

He what?

MIKE

All that stuff he was reading. He just . . . I don't know.
He got this idea. Oh, fuck, how could the stupid bastard
ever . . . shit.

RUTH

I thought you guys were going to see *Casablanca*.

MIKE

No, we had to tell you that. He had this plan. Honest to
shit, we didn't know he was serious. Him and Shelly.
We thought he's just . . . we went to the common and
he just took all his clothes off and poured gasoline all
over himself.

COOTIE

We were just shitting around, Ruth. Honest. If we
thought he was serious we'd've stopped him, you
know.

MIKE

It was that fucking Shelly.

RUTH

You fucking stupid . . .

MIKE

I'm telling you, it wasn't our fault. He wouldn't have lit
the match. I know he poured the gasoline, but he'd
never've lit the match.

BOB

He's . . .

MIKE

Oh shit, it was awful. He just sat there turning black.
I didn't want to look, but I couldn't turn away. His
skin just, Christ, it just fell away from his face and his
blood . . . [*Puts head in hand*]

RUTH

Stupid fucking guys. You should've known. Where's
Shelly?

COOTIE

She went crazy, Ruth. She just cracked up. We had to
practically knock her out. She's okay now.

[SHELLY *comes in the front door. Her eyes are closed
and her fists clenched.* RUTH *runs to her, doesn't know
what to do.*]

RUTH
Shelly, Oh, Shelly, Jesus . . .

SHELLY
[*Teeth clenched*] Fucking guys.

   [NORMAN *comes in. He's soaking wet and carries a gasoline can.* MIKE *and* COOTIE *rise.*]

MIKE
See, everything's cool now. Everybody trusts each other. That's what it's all about.

   [MIKE *smiles oddly at the others.*]

COOTIE
[*Registering it all*] Holy shit!

   [MIKE *and* COOTIE *leave the room.*]

SHELLY
[*Yells*] Creeps. [*To* RUTH] You got any first-aid stuff?

RUTH
Yeah.

   [RUTH *gets a box from the pantry. It's a huge white box with a red cross on it, obviously stolen.*]

BOB

Hey, what happened?

NORMAN

[*Sits*] I'm all right.

SHELLY

Don't talk, Norman. Would you make him some coffee?

RUTH

Yeah. Those guys said you burned yourself.

NORMAN

No, I'm okay.

[RUTH *makes coffee while* SHELLY *ties a bandage around* NORMAN's *wrist.*]

SHELLY

Sorry if this hurts. Hey, Ruth, those guys are really bastards. They gotta learn you don't joke around sometimes.

BOB

Hey, were you really gonna burn yourself?

NORMAN

Well, you know . . .

SHELLY

We were all supposed to do it. All four of us. We waited all this time for them to graduate with good grades and everything. Six months almost. I mean, like, the war could've ended. Fucking creeps. They went and put water in the gasoline can.

NORMAN

I think I might be getting a cold.

SHELLY

We're making coffee, Norman. Keep cool.

BOB

Hey, were you really serious?

NORMAN

Well, I thought, you know, with the war and everything.

SHELLY

Water, shit.

NORMAN

Well, there was some gas in that can.

SHELLY

Fucking creeps.

NORMAN

I definitely smelled some gas when I poured it over me.

SHELLY

Hold still, Norman.

NORMAN

I mean, I knew there was something wrong when I kept holding the match to my wrist and nothing happened.

SHELLY

What do you mean, nothing happened. What's wrong with you, Norman. You call that burn on your wrist nothing? It's the worst burn I ever saw. We're lucky we didn't get arrested.

NORMAN

I've seen movies of the Buddhist monks setting themselves on fire. They usually go up pretty quick in the movies. I bet it hurts a lot. My wrist really hurts.

[RUTH *brings* NORMAN *some coffee.*]

RUTH

Listen, we have to be out of here by tomorrow.

NORMAN

All right.

RUTH

Well, what are you gonna do?

177

NORMAN
I haven't thought about it too much. I thought I was going to be dead by now. I hadn't planned beyond that.

RUTH
You got a place to stay?

SHELLY
He'll stay with me.

NORMAN
Yeah, okay.

RUTH
We'll have to have a big cleanup in case Willis comes around.

NORMAN
I was thinking maybe I'll try to get back into graduate school. I'm getting sick of washing dishes.

[BOB *has been taking down his map of Europe from the wall.*]

BOB
I think I'll go to Europe.

NORMAN

I'm not really angry at Mel and Mike. In a way I'm
kind of glad I'm not dead.

SHELLY

I think those two guys are really evil.

[RUTH *goes down the hall.*]

BOB

You ever been to France?

SHELLY

I went last summer.

BOB

What's it like?

SHELLY

Shitty. They're really up-tight in France. I got busted in
Calais. Two weeks in prison with the runs. That's no
joke.

BOB

Maybe England.

NORMAN

I was in England once.

BOB
What's it like?

NORMAN
I went on a bicycle trip with the Youth Hostel
Organization. My father sent me.

BOB
How was it?

NORMAN
It was OK.

SHELLY
England's a lousy place.

NORMAN
I don't know. I met some nice people. I saw
Buckingham Palace. The food's not very good, but it
didn't rain much. I guess it was a pretty valuable
experience. I remember thinking at the time my
horizons were a lot wider after that trip. I don't
remember why I thought that. Maybe I'll go back there
one day.

BOB
Oh well, there's always Italy or Greece.

SHELLY

If you go over there, check out Algeria. Algeria's really something else.

[MR. WILLIS *opens the door.*]

WILLIS

OK if I step in? Hey, what have you done to your hand?

NORMAN

It's just a burn.

WILLIS

Too bad, huh? Look, how's about if I see everyone for a minute? Everybody here?

BOB

[*Yelling*] DICK, RUTH, MIKE, COOTIE, C'MERE A MINUTE. MR. WILLIS WANTS US.

WILLIS

Hey, hey, hey, you don't have to do that. You don't have to yell on account of me.

[*All come in.*]

Hi, how's everybody? Gettin' ready for the big day? You gonna wear them long robes and everything, hey? All

that fancy ceremony. Pretty good, huh? Listen, I just
wanna give the place a quick once-over because I'll tell
you why. I got this tenant moving in pretty soon so I
gotta be sure everything's OK. Get rid of them milk
bottles, that's the first thing, and I'll pick up the rent for
this month, OK? How 'bout this floor, huh? You gonna
finish it? Hey, I asked a question, who's supposed to be
doing this floor?

BOB

I am, Mr. Willis.

WILLIS

So how come you leave it half-finished?

BOB

Sorry, I never got the time.

WILLIS

Well you get it. I give you good money for them tiles,
put me back a hunnered bucks. How many landlords
you find'll do that?

BOB

Yeah, okay.

WILLIS

By tomorrow night, understand? Now, let's have a little
look round the place.

[WILLIS *goes down the hall followed by* BOB, RUTH, COOTIE, *and* MIKE.]

NORMAN
Mike.

[MIKE *turns.*]

Listen, I just want to tell you, I'm not angry about what happened.

MIKE
What do you mean?

SHELLY
You're a real creep pulling a trick like that.

MIKE
That's what I get for saving his life?

SHELLY
It's none of your business. It's the existential right of every living person to take his own life.

MIKE
No one's stopping you now.

NORMAN
What I wanted to say is, if you and Mel are coming

back next year to go to graduate school, maybe we can share a place. I mean, you know, I could come down here early and look around.

MIKE

You going home for the summer?

SHELLY

He's staying with me.

NORMAN

Yeah, well I might go home for a few weeks. Visit my folks. The best way is you write to my father, care of the Police Department, Buffalo County, and if I'm not at home he'll know where to forward it.

MIKE

Police Department, Buffalo County.

NORMAN

Yeah, or you can put "Commissioner of Police, Buffalo County." It'll reach him either way. Just put "Forward to Norman."

MIKE

Right. Me and Cootie'll be up in the great Northwest Territory helping dad with the furs. If you don't hear from us, just go ahead and find a place for all of us, 'cause sometimes the mail gets delayed.

NORMAN
Don't worry, I'll get a place.

MIKE
Commissioner of Police, Buffalo County.

NORMAN
That's right.

[MIKE *smiles at him, not without warmth. In come*
COOTIE, RUTH, BOB, DICK, *and* MR. WILLIS.]

WILLIS
Not bad. I'll tellya what I'll do. I'll keep the fifty-dollar
deposit for holes in the plaster and the broken window.

COOTIE
Hey, we didn't break that window. That was broken
when we moved in.

WILLIS
That's not my problem, Cootie. I keep the fifty and if
any of you guys got an objection, you want to take it up
with me, let's have it. Look, I got a living to make like
everybody else in town. Maybe you think I'm being a
rotten guy, but you wait. You go out there in the world
and you're gonna see things, you'll think old Willis was
Snow White and the Seven Dwarfs all rolled into one.
You're gonna see dishonesty, you're gonna see mean

people, you see swindlers, killers, queers, you see guys
trying to double-park on Saturday morning, you take
my word. The thing I love about you kids is you're
honest, you're direct. There's no shitting around with
you. Yeah, I know it sounds corny, but I'm gonna miss
having you guys around. You gotta save this poor
fuckin' country, and excuse my language. There was a
time, I can remember, when you paid your taxes and
you knew your money was goin' into the right things.
Good, wholesome things. Look at it nowadays. Two
blocks away there's a house full of guys known all over
the neighborhood to practice open homosexuality. Open
homosexuality two blocks away, and there's kids playing
right outside that house every day. I don't know. I'd go
jump in the lake if it wasn't for you kids. I never knew
anyone like you, and I been around, let me tellya. You
know where you are, you know where you're going, and
you know how to get there. That's never happened
before in the history of this whole fucking country. God
bless you kids, and good luck. I'll take a check for the
rent.

COOTIE
[*Sings*]
For he's a jolly good fellow,

OTHERS
[*Joining in*]
For he's a jolly good fellow,

For he's a jolly good fellow,
That nobody can deny.
That nobody can deny.
That nobody can deny.

   [*Etc., all the way through.* WILLIS *beams, entirely
   unaware of the spoof.*]

End of scene 6

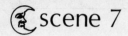# scene 7

[*The next afternoon. The kitchen is bare of furniture. The icebox is gone, only a few milk bottles left. Only one chair left.* BOB *is laying the vinyl tiles.* COOTIE *comes into the room with his* FATHER. *He grabs the last valise by the front door.*]

COOTIE
Hey, Bob, I'm going.

BOB
Yeah, we'll see you.

COOTIE
Yeah.

[MIKE *comes into the kitchen from the hall door.*]

MIKE
You going?

COOTIE
Yeah. Oh, this is my father. That's Mike, that's Bob.

BOB
Hi.

MIKE
Hi.

FATHER
A pleasure.

MIKE
What?

FATHER
It's a pleasure meeting you.

MIKE
Oh, yeah, right.

COOTIE
Well, see you guys. Hey, what you doing next year?

BOB
Oh, I got a job in a department store.

189

COOTIE
Playing piano?

BOB
Harp.

COOTIE
Great. Well, see ya.

BOB
Se ya.

MIKE
Yeah, see ya, Cootie.

FATHER
Nice meeting you boys.

[COOTIE *leaves with his* FATHER.]

MIKE
They don't look like each other. Good old Cootie. Where's Norman?

BOB
He left about an hour ago.

MIKE
Never said good-bye or anything.

BOB

You should've seen it, putting all his stuff in the back of a police car.

MIKE

What?

BOB

Yeah, his old man's Commissioner of Police, or something.

MIKE

I'll be fucked.

[RUTH *comes in from the hall with two suitcases and sets them down by some other suitcases near the door.*]

RUTH

I guess that's it. Where's Cootie?

MIKE

He just left with his dad.

RUTH

Some friend. No good-bye or anything.

MIKE

We'll see him next year.

RUTH

No we won't.

[MIKE *and* RUTH *go down the hall for their last luggage.* DICK *and the* MILKMAN *enter through the front door with empty cartons. They load the remaining bottles.*]

DICK

Hey, I wouldn't mind a little help here. I gotta catch a train.

MILKMAN

I don't understand you guys. You're supposed to be college graduates. Eight hundred and fifty-seven two-quart milk bottles. That's not the kind of thing a grown-up person does. You're supposed to be grown-ups. I don't get it.

[*The phone is ringing.*]

DICK

That's the last one.

MILKMAN

OK. I just hope you guys don't think you can go through life hoarding milk bottles like this. I got enough to do without this. I got a regular route. [*To* DICK]

Look, if you want to pick up a lot of bottles, put your fingers right down inside, you get more that way.

DICK
OK. Hey, you guys, you're a lot of help.

[MILKMAN *and* DICK *go out with their cartons.*]

BOB
[*Answering phone*] Hello, oh yes, how are you? No, this is Bob. Bob Rettie. No, music. Yes, of course I remember you. No, he's not in right now.

[MIKE *and* RUTH *have reentered, motioning* BOB *that they have to go. He motions back that it's OK. He waves good-bye as they pick up their suitcases and begin to leave.*]

RUTH
Hey, good luck.

BOB
Yeah, yeah, you too. See ya, Mike.

MIKE
See ya.

[RUTH *and* MIKE *exit through front door.*]

BOB

[*Back on phone*] Sorry, Mrs. Roper, I was just saying good-bye to some people I . . . some friends of mine. I don't know if he'll be back or not. Can I leave a message? [*Pause*] Look, Mrs. Roper, I'm very sorry about that but there's nothing I can do if he's gone. I can tell him to call you if he comes back. Mrs. Roper, look, calm down. Listen, I'm hanging up now, all right? I gotta hang up now. Good-bye, Mrs. Roper.

[BOB *hangs up and returns to the floor tiles.* DICK *comes in alone through front door.*]

DICK

Boy, that guy was sure pissed off about the bottles. You should've seen the look on his face.

BOB

Hey, you know that guy you studied with, Professor Roper?

DICK

[*Pause*] Yes.

BOB

His wife just called.

DICK

What'd she want?

BOB
She just . . . I don't know. Nothing, I guess. Pretty weird.

DICK
Yeah, pretty weird.

[DICK *puts on his coat and takes up his bags.*]

BOB
Hey, Dick.

DICK
What?

[*They look at each other.*]

BOB
I don't know. See ya.

DICK
Yeah.

[*As* DICK *is leaving, he passes a* PLUMBER.]

PLUMBER
Sorry.

[DICK *is gone through front door. The* PLUMBER *is inside.*]

Oh, brother. [*Examines the stack heater*] One of them jobs. Living, breathing, walking, talking suicide, that's what these things are. Nothing less. Boy, I haven't seen one of these things for ten years. You live here?

BOB
Yeah, sort of. I'm leaving as soon as I finish with the floor.

PLUMBER
You're lucky you're still alive with this goddamn thing. They can blow up like nobody's business. You light it with a match, am I right?

BOB
You're right.

PLUMBER
You bet I'm right. A stack heater, that's what it is, otherwise known in the trade as the suicide special number three. You forget to turn one of these things off and you wake up without a head. They got no thermostat. Nothing to shut it off when it gets too hot. Just keeps heating and heating. No wonder the guy wants a new heater.

BOB

No shit, it could really explode?

PLUMBER

Could, nothing. We used to get ten deaths a year from
these things going up. Oh yeah, they say there's
supposed to be a safety device up there in case it
overheats, but who says the safety device is gonna
work? See that doohickey up there on top? That's
what's supposed to save your life. Let's have a
chair.

[BOB *gives him the one remaining chair, which the*
PLUMBER *stands on.*]

See this copper tube? The idea's supposed to be that
when the pressure gets too high there's a little bladder
inside that ruptures, see, and the pressure comes
shooting through this copper tube into the sink. That's
why it goes into the sink. But what if the bladder don't
rupture, that's what I'm asking. The water just keeps
getting hotter and hotter by the motion of agitated
electrons skipping around from orbit to orbit and
bouncing into each other. I'm just quoting from a
chemistry book I read, I don't know if it's true or what,
could be a lot of bunk. What I'm saying is the pressure
gets too high, these here copper tanks can't hold it
in no more, and then look out. How long's this flame
been on?

BOB

I don't know. An hour or two.

PLUMBER

Lemme show you something. There's a little trip switch, you can set it off manually. You just bend the cotter pin straight and pull it out. Gotta keep your face out of the way in case of a bad fitting . . . watch . . .

[*As the* PLUMBER *says this he pulls the cotter pin and a huge jet of steam comes billowing out of the copper tube and into the sink. The steam keeps coming and coming for ages, as both stare at it. While this is happening,* KATHY *appears at the open door to the kitchen and stands looking in.* BOB *only becomes aware of her just before the* PLUMBER *begins speaking again.*]

That's what's inside there. Right, gotta get me some tools up here. If my partner turns up while I'm gone, do me a favor, willya, and tell him I gone round the corner get me a number eight pipe wrench from the pickup truck. Can you remember that?

BOB

Yeah, sure.

PLUMBER

[*Leaving*] Number eight pipe wrench. Tool of the trade. [*Sees* KATHY] Hiya, beautiful.

[*He passes by* KATHY *on the way out the front door and pats her cheek.* KATHY *comes in and walks around the kitchen.*]

KATHY
Everyone gone?

BOB
Yeah.

KATHY
Finishing the floor?

BOB
Evidently.

KATHY
Kind of late, isn't it? [*Pause*] Did they send my grades here?

BOB
On the window sill. You did really shitty.

KATHY
[*Gets the letter*] Bob, listen . . . I'm sorry about . . . sounds pretty silly.

BOB

No, I accept your apology for whatever you think you did.

KATHY

I saw Ruth the other day. She said you've been . . . well, pretty bad this semester.

BOB

Did she say that?

KATHY

I wish I'd known . . . couldn't you have . . . you should have told me to stay.

BOB

Well, it slipped my mind. Sorry.

KATHY

You shouldn't be so ashamed of your feelings.

BOB

OK.

KATHY

I'm serious. You've gotta learn to let go. Like with your music. It's all squinched and tidy.

BOB
OK. I'll work on that.

KATHY
Oh, Bob.

BOB
What?

KATHY
I really wish you'd've told me. I'd've come back. I never really related to Richard.

BOB
I'll tell him when I see him.

KATHY
Yeah, you're right. Why the hell should you be nice? Oh well, good luck . . . and, you know, when you see your mother say hello for me.

BOB
OK.

KATHY
How is she?

BOB

She's okay. Sort of dead.

KATHY

I like her, Bob. You're lucky. She's, you know, she's a real person.

BOB

No, she's, you know, a real corpse.

KATHY

All right, have it your way.

BOB

No, it's not what I wanted particularly. No, taken all in all, from various different angles, I'd've preferred it if she lived. I'm pretty sure of that.

KATHY

[*Pause*] She's not really.

BOB

School's over.

KATHY

Bob, do you know what you're saying?

BOB

Kathy, please get the fuck out of here.

KATHY

But, I mean, Ruth never told me . . . Didn't you tell anyone?

BOB

Yeah, I just told you.

KATHY

But, I mean . . . when . . . when did . . .

BOB

Christmas. No, no, it was the day after.

[KATHY *sits.*]

KATHY

Jesus, Bob, why didn't you tell anyone? I mean, how could you live for six months without telling someone?

BOB

[*With no emotion*] Oh, I don't know. A little perseverence. A little cunning. A little fortitude. [*Long pause*] They put her in this room, I don't know what you call it. They bring everyone there just before they kick the bucket. They just sort of lie around looking at each other, wondering what they got in common to talk

about. I saw her for fifteen days running. She knew. I'm
sure of that. I couldn't believe it. Not the last time
anyway. I couldn't believe that thing in bed was alive. It
was just a yellow thing. No eyes. Anyway, they drugged
her up so heavily she couldn't see anything. I think she
was trying to say something, I'm not sure. Lying there,
messing herself, rotting. There was this stuff on her
teeth. Looked like scab. Dry, greeny stuff in a sort of
web. I thought she was trying to tell me something. I
bent over to listen and caught a whiff of that breath,
like fried vomit. I was sick on her. [*Pause*] Thank Christ
she died. On the other hand, the funeral was quite a
successful affair. I didn't know she had so many friends.
It turned out the chaplain knew some of my uncle's
relatives, so we had a nice talk and he told some rotten
jokes and everyone laughed. I never got to the
graveyard. The car I was in broke down on the Merritt
Parkway. Just as well. I didn't feel like seeing all those
people again. All those . . . I never knew she had so
many friends.

KATHY
Bob . . .

BOB
Anyway, I, um, I didn't feel like talking about it. I
mean, I wasn't all that upset. I was a little upset, mostly
because I thought I ought to be more upset, but as for
your actual grief, well . . .

[KATHY *has risen.*]

Going?

[KATHY *starts out the door.*]

Give my regards to that guy you're rescuing at the moment. What's his name.

[KATHY *is gone.* BOB *shrugs. He sits. The cat comes in.*]

Hey, cat, what the fuck do you think you're doing hanging around here. All the human beings are heading west. Everyone done gone, puss-puss.

[BOB *picks up the cat and sets it outside, closing the door. He returns to his tiling. Stops and looks around. Goes to the hall door and looks down for a while, then turns back to the kitchen.*]

OK. Announcement. This really incredible thing happened to me. Hey, everyone, let me tell you about this really incredible thing that happened to me . . .

[*His body is doing something he doesn't want it to.*]

Oh fuck, come on. Shit, no, no . . .

[*But he is. He's crying, first with just his face, then*

with his whole body. His mother's death has nothing to do with it.]

End of Act Two
and of the Play